Virtual Realities

and Their Discontents

Virtual Realities
and Their Discontents

Edited by Robert Markley

The Johns Hopkins University Press
Baltimore and London

Parts of the Introduction and all of Chapters 1–5 originally
appeared in *Configurations: A Journal of Literature,
Science, and Technology* 2:3 (1994), copyright © 1994 by
The Johns Hopkins University Press and the Society for
Literature and Science.

The Johns Hopkins University Press
2715 North Charles Street
Baltimore, Maryland 21218-4319
The Johns Hopkins Press Ltd., London

ISBN 0-8018-5225-0
ISBN 0-8018-5226-9 (pbk.)

Library of Congress Cataloging-in-Publication Data will
be found at the end of this book.
A catalog record for this book is available from the
British Library.

Contents

Hayle Likes.

Acknowledgments

Any collection of essays is a collaborative
project, and this volume is no exception.
I would like to thank the following individuals for their help during the writing
and editing of *Virtual Realities and Their Discontents:* Anne Balsamo, Meredith Bricken,
Chris Byrne, Nicole DeWolf, Ken Knoespel,
Rebecca Merrens, Brian Rotman, Molly
Rothenberg, Ronald Schleifer, Steve Shaviro,
and Patrick Sheahan. Particular thanks go to
Jim Bono of *Configurations* and Eric Halpern
of the Johns Hopkins University Press,
without whom this volume might have
remained afloat in cyberspace.

Virtual Realities

and Their Discontents

Introduction:

History, Theory, and

Virtual Reality

Robert Markley

One of the ironies of our culture's fascination with virtual technologies is its fondness for consuming books and articles that proclaim the death of print culture—or its disappearance into the matrix. In one respect, the essays in this collection are dedicated to suggesting that the death of logocentrism has been greatly exaggerated. If cyberspace is the "consensual hallucination" that lies beyond the portals of virtual technologies, its means of generating that consent, as David Porush maintains in this volume, are alphabetic and mathematical schemes of representation at least three thousand years old.[1] The era of virtuality has been heralded by articles in mainstream news magazines (*Time*); special issues of scholarly journals, such as *South Atlantic Quarterly* and *Genders;* collections of essays from programmers and self-styled visionaries (*Cyberspace: First Steps*) as well as from—who else?—literary and cultural critics (*Storming the Reality Studio; Fiction 2000*); popularizations by journalists such as Howard Rheingold and Benjamin Woolley; and its own user's guide, *Mondo 2000*, something of a cross between *Rolling Stone* and *Mad* magazine.[2] Cyberspace, in short, is unthinkable without the print culture it claims to transcend. As Marshall McLuhan suggested in

1. William Gibson, *Neuromancer* (New York: Bantam, 1984), p. 7.

2. "Cyberpunk!" *Time*, February 8, 1993; *South Atlantic Quarterly* 92 (1993); *Genders* 18 (1993); Michael Benedikt, ed., *Cyberspace: First Steps* (Cambridge, Mass.: MIT Press, 1991); Larry McCaffery, ed., *Storming the Reality Studio: A Casebook of Cyberpunk and Postmodern Science Fiction* (Durham, N.C.: Duke University Press, 1991); George Slusser and Thomas Shippey, eds., *Fiction 2000* (Athens: University of Georgia Press, 1992); Howard Rheingold, *Virtual Reality* (New York: Simon and Schuster, 1991); Benjamin Woolley, *Virtual Worlds: A Journey in Hype and Hyperreality* (New York: Penguin, 1992).

the 1960s, the content of any new medium is precisely the old medium that it has replaced; and so, in McLuhan's sense, we might say that cyberspace remains fixated on the traces of the word that it ostensibly renders obsolete.[3] It is, in part, a by-product of a tradition of metaphysics which, boats against the current, bears us back relentlessly to our past.

The indebtedness of cyberspace to its logocentric past is one of the threads that ties together the essays in this collection. Another is the contributors' insistence on distinguishing, in various ways, virtual technologies (the hardware and software that intervene in our bodies) from the abstraction "cyberspace." In an important sense, it is this awareness of the historical and cultural implication of virtual technologies in the dreamscape of Western thought that sets Katherine Hayles, Richard Grusin, David Brande, David Porush, Michelle Kendrick, and me apart from those writers who characterize cyberspace as a new, if not always brave, world. The more visionary proponents and analysts of cyberspace (many of whom are discussed in the chapters of this volume) come to virtual technologies from a variety of backgrounds and perspectives, but they share the belief that cyberspace marks a revolutionary expansion—and liberation—of our senses of identity and reality. In contrast, the contributors to *Virtual Reality and Its Discontents* remain sceptical of a cyberspatial metaphysics that assumes, rather than questions, the revolutionary nature of virtual worlds and electronically mediated experience. In this respect, their analyses emphasize, albeit in different ways, that the division between cyberspace and virtual technologies reflects and reinscribes the oppositions of mind/body, spirit/matter, form/substance, and male/female that have structured Western metaphysics since Plato. To historicize and theorize virtual realities, then, is to enter into a wide-ranging investigation of technology, mathematics, economics, gender politics, and psychology that resists any simple sense of narrative or conceptual closure.

Writers on virtual technologies and cyberspace, whether proponents or sceptics, thus are drawn to the problem of definition: What, after all, counts as a virtual space? In recent years, cyberspace has become a catch-all term for everything from e-mail to GameBoy cartridges, as though each computer screen were a portal to a shadow universe of infinite, electronically accessible space. But beat to this airy thinness, cyberspace loses the specificity that supposedly

3. Marshall McLuhan, *Understanding Media: The Extensions of Man* (New York: New American Library, 1964); *The Medium Is the Message* (New York: Random House, 1967).

distinguishes it as a breakthrough in human and cultural evolution. Michael Benedikt defines cyberspace as "a globally networked, computer-sustained, computer-accessed, and computer-generated, multidimensional, artificial, or 'virtual' reality."[4] Marcos Novak draws together a composite definition: "Cyberspace is a completely spatialized visualization of all information in global information processing systems, along pathways provided by present and future communication networks, enabling full copresence and interaction of multiple users, allowing input and output from and to the full human sensorium, permitting simulations of real and virtual realities, remote data collection and control through telepresence, and total integration and intercommunication with a full range of intelligent products and environments in real space." This hardwired universe of simulated experience, though, is more than the sum of its parts: "Cyberspace is a habitat of the imagination, a habitat for the imagination . . . the place where conscious dreaming meets subconscious dreaming, a landscape of rational magic, of mystical reason, the locus and triumph of poetry over poverty, of 'it-can-be-so' over 'it-should-be-so.'"[5] The transition from the rhetoric of technocorporatism to a romanticism filtered through *Star Trek* reruns is less abrupt than it seems. The rhetoric of cyberspace characteristically invokes the pleasure and power of an imaginative world made whole, as Novak's emphasis (drawn in part from cyberpunk novelist Bruce Sterling) on fullness, plenitude, and mystical unity suggests.

The crucial metaphors used to evoke cyberspace, then, are self-consciously holistic, transcendent, sublime; they attempt to describe our "full human sensorium" beyond Freudian repression or Marxian alienation, to liberate our "imagination"—"poetry"—from the constraints of material existence—"poverty." Even scientists who are dedicated to promoting virtual technologies in fields such as medicine drift into a metaphysically laden rhetoric that equates poetry with an escape from the history that has brought these technologies into being. The flight into an imaginary space collapses distinctions among technological innovation, artistic creativity, and politico-economic power. Richard M. Satava of the Advanced Research Projects Agency (and a major figure in the development of virtual technologies for laparoscopic surgery) declares that "the video monitor is [becoming] the portal into the entire world of information; this 'electronic interface' will bestow power beyond

4. Benedikt, *Cyberspace* (above, n. 2), p. 122.

5. Marcos Novak, "Liquid Architecture in Cyberspace," in ibid., pp. 225, 226.

imagination."[6] Although it might be tempting to dwell on the militaristic overtones of Satava's rhetoric, the significant point about his pronouncement is that it describes the ends of virtual technologies—"The King is Dead"—in metaphors which suggest, as Porush contends, that our consciousness itself is always and already mediated by the interventions of print and number, neurotechnologies which mark it irrevocably as metaphoric. Paradoxically, Benedikt, Novak, and Satava demonstrate that virtual technologies must invoke "poetry"—a tradition of idealization and hierarchical values—in order to acknowledge and repress the sustenance they require from a contentious metaphysics. Cyberspace, then, can never separate itself from the politics of representation precisely because it is a projection of the conflicts of class, gender, and race that technology both encodes and seeks to erase. It does not transcend the dead body of the king—"the future," says Satava, "holds [the] promise of a virtual cadaver nearly indistinguishable from a real person"[7]—but reinscribes the profit-based politics of accelerating and intensifying interventions in living bodies.

Technology never escapes politics. The fiction of cyberspace is useful precisely to the extent that it allows its proponents to imagine an androcentric reality in which a threatening, messy, or recalcitrant (and invariably feminized) nature never intrudes. In this respect, cyberspace is consensual primarily in its insistence that technologically mediated experience can transcend the ecological and economic constraints that have shaped and continue to shape human culture. It offers the fantasy that the more technologically sophisticated our society becomes the less it has to worry about the distribution of wealth and resources. In his characterization of postindustrialism, Benedikt asserts that "the economic principles of material production and distribution in their classically understood forms—principles of property, wealth, markets, capital, and labor—are no longer sufficient to describe or guide the dynamics of our modern, complex, 'information' society."[8] The claims for the revolutionary nature of cyberspace, for its "mystical reason," are compelling to many because they offer a short cut to the land of plenty: in cyberspace, scarce resources become infinite possibilities. But as Brande argues in his essay, the transformation of modes of produc-

6. Richard M. Satava, "Medicine 2001: The King Is Dead," in Richard M. Satava, Karen Morgan, Hans B. Sieburg, Rudy Mattheus, and Jens P. Christensen, eds., *Interactive Technology and the New Paradigm for Healthcare* (Amsterdam: IOS Press, 1995), p. 335.

7. Satava, "Medicine 2001," p. 337.

8. Benedikt, *Cyberspace* (above, n. 2), p. 121.

tion and distribution does not mean that the problems of capitalism disappear; and, as Grusin suggests, simply invoking "information" as the evolutionary successor of "writing" does little to alter the politics of symbolic, or monetary, accumulation. One of the abiding fictions of cyberspace—of all technologies, really—is that it can cut rather than untie the knot of present-day problems. In this respect, cyberspace gives a new form to an age-old dream: that through our ingenuity humanity can devise products and riches in excess of the resources required to manufacture and maintain them.

A case in point: in November of 1994, I participated in Green-Space, a real-time Virtual Reality link between the Human Interface Technology Laboratory at the Washington Technology Center in Seattle and the NICOGRAPH (Nippon Computer Graphics) trade show in Tokyo. The University of Washington weekly, *University Week,* described the trial run as follows:

> [Four] persons [two in Tokyo, two in Seattle] donned head-mounted video displays and came together in specifically created virtual meeting rooms equipped with either Occidental or Oriental furnishings [Mt. Ranier was visible in Tokyo; I sat in the cartoon graphic shadow of Mt. Fuji], suggesting that they traveled to the network's other shore. However, participants got the impression that everyone was in the same room sitting around the same conference table. They then played a short, interactive game in which creatures materialized that only can be captured with the cooperation of two or more participants using conventional hand-movement tracking devices.[9]

In reality (pardon the pun), I watched the digitalized face of one of my colleagues run in a loop through five facial expressions across a virtual table. Neither we nor the virtually present Japanese faces to our sides had any visible success in swatting the bouncing cartoon creatures into one of the four billiard-like pockets at the corners of the conference table. My experience of this "new era in teleconferencing" (funded, in part, by the Fujitsu Research Center in Japan) suggests that GreenSpace is more a political metaphor than a technological breakthrough. Even if the sound hookup had worked, I do not speak Japanese, and the "cooperation" that was supposed to take place was undone because all four of us were proprioceptively disoriented, a common experience in virtual worlds that lack force feedback mechanisms. If one imagines a future in which representatives of the institutions financing GreenSpace meet virtually to swat at Third World countries or redundant workers, virtual teleconferencing could easily put a dent in transoceanic travel for corporate

9. *University Week,* November 17, 1994, p. 1.

executives. But this application of virtual technologies, it should be obvious, reinscribes rather than revolutionizes the economic power that advanced telecommunications represents. To make this statement is not to attack the potential of these technologies but to recognize that their content is the previous medium—in this instance, long distance communication—that it subsumes and recodes. The conference itself becomes the product to be disseminated rather than a means to an end. In GreenSpace, talk isn't cheap.

The unintended legacy of commodifying face-to-face conversation, though, may be to force our culture to assess the consequences of its investments in a dualistic metaphysics that divorces mind from body and that sees technology as a mere tool to be manipulated rather than as a process that disrupts and reconfigures whatever we take to be "essentially" human. As a projection of the imaginary spaces that structure our self-perceptions, our self-consciousness, cyberspace relies for its symbolic coherence on a narrative logic of progress which underwrites and transcends individual agency or intention.[10] It offers itself as the logical *telos* of technological progress. To create a history of and for cyberspace, writers such as Howard Rheingold and Benjamin Woolley describe key episodes in the development of computer technology, link them in a more-or-less causal sequence, and then extend this narrative into an imagined future. If we read our recent computer-aided past as the progress of protovirtual technologies, then it becomes easy to imagine Virtual Reality as the logical outcome of our efforts, the fulfillment of a quest for a postindustrial, postmodern transcendence, the ascent to a Leibnizian future in which the body (suitably dematerialized) becomes indistinguishable from its idealized simulation.[11]

10. See Larry Laudan, "Progress of Rationality? The Prospects for a Normative Naturalism," *American Philosophical Quarterly* 24 (1987), esp. p. 28; and Joseph Rouse, "Philosophy of Science and the Persistent Narratives of Modernity," *Studies in the History and Philosophy of Science* 22 (1991), esp. pp. 157–162.

11. Within a week of the initial appearance of the article included below (in the fall 1994 issue of *Configurations*), I received a half-dozen letters or e-mail messages from computer programmers, mathematicians, and one literary theorist, all of whom questioned my characterization of Leibniz. To reply to their queries would require another article (at least) and take us deep into the heart of a debate about the ways in which "the body" has been celebrated in and erased from both Western philosophy and recent cultural criticism. In brief, as I suggest below, Leibniz has emerged as the guru of cyberspatial metaphysics precisely because his monadology offers a means to preserve a logic of simulation in which an embodied individual can project herself as a kind of seemingly pure desire into cyberspace: agency without consequences. In a provocative move, Michelle Kendrick, in her essay in this collection, argues that it may be the sceptical philosopher of experience, David Hume, rather than Leibniz who offers us

In its quest to find a suitable past from which virtual realities can claim descent, Rheingold's *Virtual Reality* details the history of interactive technologies, ranging from Morton Heilig's Sensorama in the 1950s, to video games, to experimental programs in California and North Carolina. As his narrative unfolds, Rheingold crisscrosses the country, talking to computer programmers, entrepreneurs, and groupies, including veterans of the retro-sixties subculture such as Timothy Leary and Jerry Garcia, who is credited with one of the dust-jacket blurbs on the back cover of *Virtual Reality:* "They made LSD illegal. I wonder what they're going to do about this stuff." Woolley's *Virtual Worlds* is, if anything, more eclectic: intermixed with histories of computing, flight simulators, hypertext, and graphic displays are thumbnail sketches of numerous modernist and postmodernist thinkers—from Leary, to Fredric Jameson, to Roland Barthes, to Jean Baudrillard. As his subtitle, *A Journey in Hype and Hyperreality,* suggests, Woolley analyzes the potential of Virtual Reality in the generic form of a travelogue, a picaresque account of various approaches to simulation and simulacra, to the redefinition of "reality" at the end of the twentieth century. For Rheingold and Woolley, the history of interactive technologies is necessarily inclusive. Because "Virtual Reality" seeks to mimic the complexity of proprioceptive experience, it becomes an imperialistic metaphor, a textual black hole, that encourages Rheingold and Woolley to include anything they want in their narratives. Ironically, they demonstrate that Virtual Reality remains a semiotic fiction: to immerse oneself in a fully credible "reality," one needs to imagine a simulated world every bit as complex as the "real" world it tries to represent. This endless expanse of imagined terrain, as Porush suggests, is the metaphysical ghost haunting postmodern technologies.

In different ways, the contributors to this collection reexamine this history—the metanarrative of technological development—on which millenarian visions of cyberspace rely. Taking a variety of approaches, they explore the ways in which virtual realities conserve and incorporate rather than overthrow the assumptions and values of a traditional, logocentric humanism, the Platonist division of the world into the physical and metaphysical in which ideal forms are valued over material content. Cyberspace, Porush suggests, represents not a break with our metaphysical past but an extension of its

the ur-logic of virtual technologies. In a Humean framework, virtuality emerges not as a space in which to distill and conserve a holistic identity but as a testing ground for a series of noncausal, seemingly arbitrary experiences whose connection to "reality" remains always problematic, always in need of articulation. Virtual Reality is to "real" reality, then, as a surgical simulation is to an actual operation.

basic theistic postulates. Grusin argues that the claims for new
forms of electronic communication depend on the very notions of
authorship—and subjectivity—which they claim to transcend. In
her essay, Hayles examines debates about cybernetics at the Macy
conferences in the 1950s to demonstrate that the history of mind-
body ideas in the age of computers and feedback loops is itself conflicted and that these conflicts inform current debates about Virtual
Reality. Brande analyzes cyberspace as an extension of the logic of
late twentieth-century capitalism, suggesting that the fiction of
William Gibson, in particular, plays a crucial role in theorizing the
implications of the information revolution. Kendrick explores the
consequences of inhabiting simulated worlds, by discussing a case
of rape in a text-based virtual environment. Drawing on the writ-
ings of some key figures in the development of virtual technologies,
I examine the entangled roots of cyberspace in the philosophy of
mathematics, or, more precisely, in a particular reading of the philosophy of mathematics, one which privileges idealist descriptions
of the universe. As different as these approaches may seem, they
share a scepticism about our new postindustrial metaphysics. Taken
together, they explore the implications of a philosophy of virtuality
which perceives the universe as ultimately computable, an effort to
render "reality" an effect of the "virtual" world of mathematics. In
its quest for a transcendent formal integrity, cyberspace seems analogous to the mathematical models of, say, superstring theory: it asserts the existence of a fundamental reality of form underlying our
mundane existence, a reality sanctified by the elegant formalism of
a mathematics that we must accept, finally, because it offers us a
world more aesthetically pleasing, more beautiful, than the one we
inhabit.

Proponents of virtual technologies, of course, argue that such dualisms can be overcome or that cyberspace represents an evolution
beyond the opposition of physics and metaphysics. Benedikt, for
example, suggests that cyberspace mediates between the ethereal
and the concrete; it describes, he contends, "a new niche for a realm
that lies between the . . . worlds" of thought and body.[12] But even if
we see cyberspace as a form of complex mediation within the traditions of Western science, metaphysics, and economics, it does not
transcend the problems of materiality, embodiment, or capital. In
this regard, to offer a critique of cyberspace is to engage in a multivalent exploration of the values and assumptions of a dualism
which are presented as "natural" conditions of human existence, of

12. Benedikt, *Cyberspace* (above, n. 2), p. 124.

an ideology of a revolutionary change in consciousness brought about by new forms of technological intervention, and of the political problems posed by limited access to new and expensive technologies. Important challenges to the politics of information technologies have emerged in recent years, even as Jerry Garcia has been enlisted to portray Virtual Reality as a countercultural phenomenon.[13] What the contributors to *Virtual Realities and Their Discontents* suggest is that this political critique of cyberspace cannot be limited to the problems of access but must engage in a sceptical treatment of the rhetoric of the "new" that is endemic to both academic and popular writing on cyberspace, postmodernism, and late capitalism. The blind spot of many critics of virtual technologies lies in their tacit acceptance of progress as natural, as inevitable, and their casual assumption that we are living in revolutionary times in which technology intervenes in our subjectivity in ways undreamt of before the late twentieth century. This is the approach of such philosophers as Michael Heim, who traces the morphogenesis of cyberspace back to Leibniz's monadology, of graphic artists such as Nicole Stenger, and of educators such as Meredith Bricken.[14] To be sure, these writers recognize that political problems exist in terms of access to cyberspace, but they limit the nature of those problems— accepting the "revolutionary" nature of interventionist technologies, then suggesting that we need to find ways to time-share our rides on the whirlwind.

If Virtual Reality is already a battleground for control of the cyborg as metaphor and as moneymaker, its battle lines are multiple and fractured, and the contending forces are characterized by shifting alliances and conflicting investments. Cyberspace is irrevocably marked by competing values and assumptions about reality and subjectivity, by previous political struggles to naturalize and resist particular constructions of reality. But this recognition is only the beginning of an analysis of the era of virtuality. As cultural critics of science, we need to familiarize ourselves with the technological innovations described six times a year in *CyberEdge*, "The World's Leading Newsletter of Virtual Reality"; we need to explore the venture capitalist realm of such companies as High Techsplanations,

13. See, for example, Gary Chapman, "Taming the Computer," *South Atlantic Quarterly* 92 (1993): 681–712; and Kathleen Biddick, "Humanist History and the Haunting of Virtual Worlds: Problems of Memory and Rememoration," *Genders* 18 (1993): 47–66.

14. Michael Heim, *The Metaphysics of Cyberspace* (New York: Oxford University Press, 1993); Nicole Stenger, "Mind Is a Leaking Rainbow," in Benedikt, *Cyberspace* (above, n. 2), pp. 49–58; and Meredith Bricken, "Virtual Worlds: No Interface to Design," in ibid., pp. 363–382.

Immersion Corporation, and Boston Dynamics, which are now marketing surgical simulation equipment with force feedback mechanisms; and, most importantly, we need to recognize that there are
potential allies as well as antagonists who work within the complicated webs of technology and capital that define the business of
Virtual Reality.[15] It is only by understanding virtual technologies
within the histories that cyberspace seeks to deny or transcend that
we can begin to dream a different kind of "real."

15. See, for example, Jonathan R. Merril, "Surgery on the Cutting Edge: Virtual Reality
Applications in Medical Education," *Virtual Reality World,* November–December 1993,
pp. 17–21.

Boundary Disputes: Homeostasis, Reflexivity, and the Foundations of Cybernetics

N. Katherine Hayles

Virtual reality did not spring, like Athena from the forehead of Zeus, full-blown from the mind of William Gibson. It has encoded within it a complex history of technological innovations, conceptual developments, and metaphorical linkages that are crucially important in determining how it will develop and what it is taken to signify. This essay explores that history by focusing on certain developments within cybernetics from the immediate post–World War II period to the present. These developments can be understood as progressing in three waves. The first period, 1945–1960, marks the foundational stage during which cybernetics was forged as an interdisciplinary framework that would allow humans, animals, and machines to be constituted through the common denominators of feedback loops, signal transmission, and goal-seeking behavior. The forum for these developments was a series of conferences sponsored by the Josiah Macy Foundation between 1946 and 1953.[1] Through the Macy discussions and the research presented there, the discipline solidified around key concepts and was disseminated into American intellectual communities by Macy

1. Five of the Macy Conference transactions were published under the title *Cybernetics: Circular Causal and Feedback Mechanisms in Biological and Social Systems*, vols. 6–10, ed. Heinz von Foerster (New York: Macy Foundation, 1949–1955) (hereinafter cited as *Cybernetics*, with conference number and year). The best study of the Macy conferences is Steve J. Heims, *The Cybernetics Group* (Cambridge, Mass.: MIT Press, 1991); in addition to discussing the conferences, Heims also conducted interviews with many of the participants who have since died.

conferees, guests, and fellow travelers. Humans and machines had been equated for a long time, but it was largely through the Macy conferences that both were understood as information-processing systems.

Although space will not permit me to develop the second and third waves in detail, a synopsis will be useful in understanding the connections between them and later developments in virtual reality. The second wave was initiated by Heinz von Foerster, an Austrian émigré who became the coeditor of the Macy transcripts. This phase can be dated from 1960, when a collection of von Foerster's essays appeared under the title *Observing Systems*.[2] "Second-order cybernetics," von Foerster called the models he presented in these essays, because they extended cybernetic principles to the cyberneticians who had devised the principles. As his punning title recognizes, the observer of systems can himself be constituted as a system to be observed. The second wave reached its mature phase with Humberto Maturana's *Autopoiesis and Cognition*, coauthored with Francisco Varela.[3] Maturana and Varela developed von Foerster's self-reflexive emphasis into a radical epistemology that saw the world as a set of formally closed systems. Organisms respond to their environment in ways determined by their internal self-organization. Hence they are not only self-organizing, they are also autopoietic, or self-making. Through the work of Maturana, Varela, and such theorists as the German sociologist Niklas Luhmann,[4] by 1980 cybernetics had moved from an umbrella term covering a collection of related concepts to a coherent theory undergirding the claims of a sophisticated and controversial epistemology.

The third wave emerged when virtual reality, combining the idea of a feedback loop with the greatly increased power of microcomputers, began to enter professional and consumer marketplaces with immersive devices that spliced the user's sensorium into three-dimensional simulated worlds. Instantiating the formal closure that Maturana saw as the basis for all perception in the closed loop that runs from the user's body through the simulation, VR technologies

2. Heinz von Foerster, *Observing Systems*, 2nd ed. (Salinas: Intersystems Publications, 1984).

3. Humberto R. Maturana and Francisco J. Varela, *Autopoiesis and Cognition: The Realization of the Living*, Boston Studies in the Philosophy of Science, vol. 42 (Dordrecht: D. Reidel, 1980).

4. Niklas Luhmann has modified and extended Maturana's epistemology in significant ways; see, for example, his *Essays on Self-Reference* (New York: Columbia University Press, 1990) and "The Cognitive Program of Constructivism and a Reality that Remains Unknown," in *Selforganization: Portrait of a Scientific Revolution*, ed. Wolfgang Krohn et al. (Dordrecht: Kluwer Academic Publishers, 1990), pp. 64–85.

provided a phenomenology to go along with the epistemology of autopoiesis. In the third wave, the idea of a virtual world of information that coexists with and interpenetrates the material world of objects is no longer an abstraction. It has come home to roost, so to speak, in the human sensorium itself.

Half a century beyond the watershed of the Macy conferences, feedback loops have become household words and cybernouns are breeding like flies, spawning cybernauts, cyberfutures, and cyber-sluts. People no longer find it strange to think of material objects as informational patterns. Hans Moravec, head of the Carnegie-Mellon Mobile Robot Laboratory, has even proposed a visionary scenario in which human consciousness is transformed into an informational pattern, extracted from the brain, and downloaded into a computer. [5] If there was ever a case to be made for a paradigm shift, this would seem to be it. Yet a close examination of threads in this tangled skein does not bear out either Kuhn's model of a revolutionary break or Foucault's vision of a new episteme springing suddenly into being across a wide range of cultural sites. Rather, the changes appear to be much more like what archeological anthropologists find when they study material culture: instead of a sudden break, change came about through overlapping patterns of innovation and replication. Part of my argument is thus historical, focusing on the specificities of how change occurred during the foundational period of cybernetics. Part of it is synthetic and conceptual, concerned to develop a schematic that will show how the three waves relate to each other (see Figure 1). The schematic illustrates the traffic between ideas and artifacts, suggesting that concepts, like artifacts, embody sedimented histories that affect how they develop. To make this argument, I will introduce a triad of terms appropriated from studies of material culture: seriation, skeuomorphs, and conceptual constellations. Finally, I will use this model of historical change to interrogate why it seems possible, at this cultural moment, for virtuality to displace materiality. I will argue that the claim for the self-sufficiency of a virtual world of information is deeply problematic, for this illusion, like everything that exists, has its basis in the very materiality it would deny.

Seriation, Skeuomorphs, and Conceptual Constellations

In archeology, changes in artifacts are customarily mapped through seriation charts. One may construct a seriation chart by parsing an artifact as a set of attributes that change over time. One

5. Hans Moravec, *Mind Children: The Future of Robot and Human Intelligence* (Cambridge, Mass.: Harvard University Press, 1988), pp. 109–110.

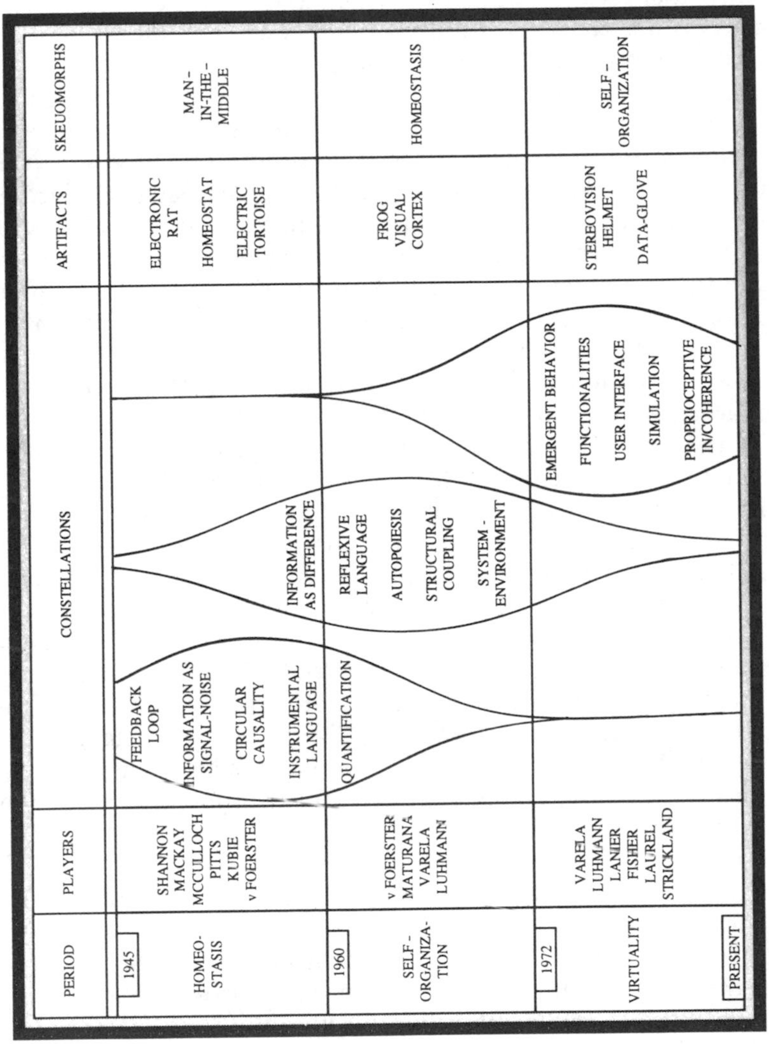

PERIOD	PLAYERS	CONSTELLATIONS	ARTIFACTS	SKEUOMORPHS
1945 HOMEO-STASIS	SHANNON MACKAY MCCULLOCH PITTS KUBIE v FOERSTER	FEEDBACK LOOP INFORMATION AS SIGNAL-NOISE CIRCULAR CAUSALITY INSTRUMENTAL LANGUAGE QUANTIFICATION	ELECTRONIC RAT HOMEOSTAT ELECTRIC TORTOISE	MAN-IN-THE-MIDDLE
1960 SELF-ORGANIZA-TION	v FOERSTER MATURANA VARELA LUHMANN	INFORMATION AS DIFFERENCE REFLEXIVE LANGUAGE AUTOPOIESIS STRUCTURAL COUPLING SYSTEM-ENVIRONMENT	FROG VISUAL CORTEX	HOMEOSTASIS
1972 VIRTUALITY	VARELA LUHMANN LANIER FISHER LAUREL STRICKLAND	EMERGENT BEHAVIOR FUNCTIONALITIES USER INTERFACE SIMULATION PROPRIOCEPTIVE IN/COHERENCE	STEREOVISION HELMET DATA-GLOVE	SELF-ORGANIZATION
PRESENT				

Figure 1.

14

of the attributes of a lamp, for example, is the element that gives off light. The first lamps used wicks for this element. Later, with the discovery of electricity, wicks gave way to filaments. The figures that customarily emerge from this kind of analysis are shaped like a tiger's iris—narrow at the top when an attribute first begins to be introduced, with a bulge in the middle during an attribute's heyday, tapering off at the bottom as the shift to a new model is completed. On a seriation chart for lamps, a line drawn at 1890 would show the figure for wicks waxing large, while the figure showing filaments would be intersected at the narrow tip of the top end; fifty years later, the wick figure would be tapering off, while the filament figure would be widening into its middle section. Considered as a set, the figures depicting changes in an artifact's attributes reveal patterns of overlapping innovation and replication. Some attributes are changed from one model to the next, while others remain essentially the same.

As Figure 1 suggests, the conceptual shifts that took place during the development of cybernetics display a pattern of overlapping innovation and replication reminiscent of material changes in artifacts. It is not surprising that conceptual fields should evolve similarly to material culture, for concept and artifact engage each other in continuous feedback loops. An artifact materially expresses the concept it embodies, but the process of its construction is far from passive. A glitch has to be fixed, a material exhibits unexpected properties, an emergent behavior surfaces—any of these challenges can give rise to a new concept, which results in another generation of artifact, which leads to the development of still other concepts. The reasoning suggests that it should be possible to construct a seriation chart tracing the development of a conceptual field analogous to seriation charts for artifacts.

In the course of the Macy conferences, certain ideas came to be associated with each other. Through a cumulative process that continued across several years of discussions, they were seen as mutually entailing each other until, like love and marriage, it seemed natural to the participants that they should go together. Such a constellation is the conceptual entity corresponding to an artifact, possessing an internal coherence that defines it as an operational unit. Its formation marks the beginning of a period; its disassembly and reconstruction, the transition to a different period. Indeed, periods are recognizable as such largely because constellations possess this coherence. Rarely is a constellation discarded wholesale; rather, some of the ideas comprising it are discarded, others are modified, and new ones are introduced. Like the attributes that comprise an artifact, the ideas in a constellation change in a patchwork pattern of old and new.

During the Macy conferences, two constellations formed that were in competition with one another. One of these was deeply conservative, privileging constancy over change, predictability over complexity, equilibrium over evolution. At the center of this constellation was the concept of homeostasis, defined as the ability of an organism to maintain itself in a stable state. The other constellation led away from the closed circle of corrective feedback, privileging change over constancy, evolution over equilibrium, complexity over predictability. The central concept embedded in it was reflexivity, which for our purposes can be defined as turning a system's rules back on itself so as to cause it to engage in more complex behavior. In broader social terms, homeostasis reflected the desire for a "return to normalcy" after the maelstrom of World War II. By contrast, reflexivity pointed toward the open horizon of an unpredictable and increasingly complex postmodern world.

Around these two central concepts accreted a number of related ideas, like clumps of barnacles around the first mollusks brave enough to fasten themselves to a rock. Because the two constellations were in competition, each tended to define itself as what the other was not. They were engaged, in other words, in what Derrida has called an economy of supplementarity: the necessity *not* to be what the other *was* helped to define each partner in the dialectic. The reflexivity constellation, more amorphous and fuzzily defined than was homeostasis during the Macy period, finally collapsed as a viable model. At that point its homeostatic partner could not maintain itself in isolation, and out of this chaos a new constellation began to form through a seriated pattern of overlapping innovation and replication, taking elements from both of its predecessors and adding new features as well. This diachronic movement out of the homeostasis/reflexivity dialectic marks the end of the first wave of cybernetics.

Here I want to introduce another term from archeological anthropology. A skeuomorph is a design feature, no longer functional in itself, that refers back to an avatar that was functional at an earlier time. The dashboard of my Toyota Camry, for example, is covered by vinyl molded to simulate stitching; the simulated stitching alludes back to a fabric that was in fact stitched, although it no longer serves that function in my car. Skeuomorphs visibly testify to the social or psychological necessity for innovation to be tempered by replication. Like anachronisms, their pejorative first cousins, skeuomorphs are not unusual. On the contrary, they are so deeply characteristic of the way concepts and artifacts evolve that it takes a great deal of conscious effort to avoid them. At Siggraph 93, the annual conference on computer graphics that showcases new products, I saw more skeuomorphs than morphs.

Perhaps the wittiest of these skeuomorphs was the "Catholic Turing Test" simulation, complete with a bench where the supplicant could kneel while making a confession by choosing selections from the video screen.[6] How can I understand the pleasure I took in this display? On one level, the installation alluded to the triumph of science over religion, for the role of divinely authorized interrogation and absolution had been taken over by a machine algorithm. On another level, the installation pointed to the intransigence of conditioned behavior, for the machine's form and function were determined by its religious precedessor. Like a Janus figure, the skeuomorph can look to both past and future, simultaneously reinforcing and undermining both. It calls into a play a psychodynamic that finds the new more acceptable when it recalls the old that it is in the process of displacing, and the traditional more comfortable when it is presented in a context that reminds us we can escape from it into the new. In the history of cybernetics, skeuomorphs acted as threshold devices, smoothing the transition between one conceptual constellation and another. Homeostasis, a foundational concept during the first wave, functions during the second wave as a skeuomorph. Although it is carried over into the new constellation, it ceases to be an initiating premise and instead performs the work of a gesture or an allusion used to authenticate the new elements in the emerging constellation. At the same time, it also exerts an inertial pull on the new elements that limits how radically they can transform the constellation.

A similar phenomenon appears in the transition from the second to the third wave. Reflexivity, the key concept of the second wave, is displaced in the third wave by emergence. Like homeostasis, reflexivity does not altogether disappear but lingers on as an allusion that authenticates new elements. It performs a more complex role than mere nostalgia, however, for it also leaves its imprint on the new constellation in the possibility that the virtual space can close on itself to create an autopoietic world sufficient unto itself, independent of the larger reality in which it is embedded. The complex story formed by these seriated changes between the three

6. The simulation is the creation of Gregory P. Garvey of Concordia University. An account of it can be found in *Visual Proceedings: The Art and Interdisciplinary Programs of Siggraph 93*, ed. Thomas E. Linehan (New York: Association for Computing Machinery, 1993), p. 125.

waves begins when humans and machines are equated by defining both as information-processing systems. If information is the link connecting humans and machines, then how it is defined is crucial. It is through this struggle that the first set of constellations is forged.

The Meaning of Information

From the beginning, "information" was a contested term. At issue was whether it should be defined solely as a mathematical function, without reference to its meaning to a receiver, or whether it should be linked to the context in which it is received and understood. The principal spokesperson for the mathematical definition was Claude Shannon, the brilliant electrical engineer at Bell Laboratories who formulated information as a function of the probability distribution of the elements comprising the message.[7] Shannon went out of his way to point out that this definition of information divorces it from the common understanding of information as conveying meaning. Information theory as Shannon developed it has only to do with the efficient transmission of messages through communication channels, not with what messages mean. Although others were quick to impute larger linguistic and social implications to his theory, Shannon was reluctant to generalize beyond the specialized denotation that information had within the context of electrical engineering. Responding to a presentation by Alex Bavelas on group communication at the eighth Macy conference, Shannon cautioned that he did not see "too close a connection between the notion of information as we use it in communication engineering and what you are doing here . . . the problem here is not so much finding the best encoding of symbols . . . but, rather, the determination of the semantic question of what to send and to whom to send it."[8] For Shannon, defining information was a strategic choice that enabled him to bracket semantics. He especially did not want to get involved in having to consider the receiver's mindset as part of the communication system. So strongly did he feel on the point that he suggested Bavelas distinguish between information in a channel and information in a human mind by characterizing the latter through "subjective probabilities," although how these were to be defined and calculated was by no means clear.

Donald MacKay took the opposite view, using his privileges as a

7. An account of Shannon's theory can be found in Claude E. Shannon and Warren Weaver, *The Mathematical Theory of Communication* (Urbana: University of Illinois Press, 1949).

8. *Cybernetics* (Eighth Conference, 1952), p. 22.

guest lecturer at the Macy conferences to argue for a close connection between information and meaning. In the rhetoric of the conferences, "objective" was associated with being "scientific," whereas "subjective" was a code word implying that one had fallen into a morass of unquantifiable feelings that might be magnificent but were certainly not science. MacKay's first move was to rescue information affecting the receiver's mindset from the "subjective" label. He proposed that both Shannon and Bavelas were concerned with what he called "selective information"—that is, information calculated by considering the selection of message elements from a set. MacKay argued for another kind of information that he called "structural": structural information has the capacity to "increase the number of dimensions in the information space" by acting as a metacommunication.[9]

To illustrate the distinction, say I launch into a joke and it falls flat; in that case, I may resort to telling my interlocutor, "That was a joke." The joke's message content, considered as selective information, can be calculated as a function of the probabilities of the message elements. Performing this calculation is equivalent to operating within a two-dimensional space, for the only variables are the probability and probability function. By contrast, my comment identifying the message as a joke is structural information, for it implies the existence of two different kinds of messages—jokes and serious statements. To accommodate this distinction, another parameter is necessary. This parametric variation can be represented by stacking two planes on top of one another, with the vertical dimension expressing the relation between the two types of information. Other kinds of metacommunications—for example, comments distinguishing between literal and metaphoric statements—would add additional parameters and more stacks. In another image that MacKay liked to use, he envisioned selective information as choosing among folders in a file drawer, whereas structural information increased the number of drawers.

Since structural information amounts to information on how to interpret a message, the effect on the receiver necessarily enters the picture. By calling such information "structural" rather than "subjective," MacKay changed its connotation. Not only did "structural" remove the suggestion of unscientific subjectivity, it also elevated the noun it modified to the status of a metacommunication that controls the subsystem with which it communicates. Thus the

9. Donald M. MacKay, "In Search of Basic Symbols," in *Cybernetics* (Eighth Conference, 1952), pp. 181–221. A fuller account can be found in Donald M. MacKay, *Information, Mechanism, and Meaning* (Cambridge, Mass.: MIT Press, 1969).

move from "subjective" to "structural" information made a negatively encoded term into a positive position of power. In a sense, of course, he was doing no more than any good rhetorician would—choosing his words carefully so they produced the desired effect in his audience. But entwined with this rhetorical effect was a model that triangulated between reflexivity, information, and meaning. Arguing for a strong correlation between the *nature* of a representation and its *effect*, his argument recognized the mutual constitution of language and content, message and receiver.

The problem was how to quantify the model. It implied that representations have a double valence: seen in one perspective, they are measuring instruments that point out into the world; in another perspective, they point back to the human agents who created them. By registering changes in the measuring instruments, one can infer something about the mental states of the agents who made them. And how does one perform this calculation? Through changes in an observing mind, which in turn can also be observed and measured by another mind. The progression inevitably turns into the infinite regress characteristic of reflexivity. This kind of move is familiar in twentieth-century art and literature, from the drawings of M. C. Escher to the fictions of Borges. Indeed, it is hardly an exaggeration to say that it has become an artistic and critical commonplace. Finding it in a quantitative field like information theory is more unusual. In the context of the Macy conferences, MacKay's conclusion qualified as radical: reflexivity, far from being a morass to be avoided, is precisely what enables information and meaning to be connected.

To achieve quantification, however, it was necessary to have a mathematical model for the changes the message triggered in the receiver's mind. The staggering problems this presented no doubt explain why MacKay's version of information theory was not widely accepted among the electrical engineers who would be writing, reading, and teaching the textbooks on information theory in the coming decades. Historically it was Shannon's definition of information, not MacKay's, that became the industry standard. The issues underlying the debate between Shannon and MacKay are important for the Macy conferences, for they instantiate a central problem faced by the participants. Throughout the transcripts, there is constant tension between the desire to define problems narrowly so that reliable quantification could be achieved, and the desire to define them broadly so that they could address the momentous questions that kept edging their way into the discussions. These conflicting desires kept getting tangled up with each other. On the one hand, broad implications were drawn from narrowly constructed problems. On the other, problems constructed so broadly that they were unworkable quantitatively were nevertheless treated as if they were viable scientific models. The discrepancy led Steve Heims, in his study of the Macy conferences, to remark that much of the "so-called social science was unconvincing to me as science in any traditional sense. In fact, some of it seemed to have only a thin scientific veneer, which apparently sufficed to make it acceptable."[10]

My interest in this tension has a different focus. I want to show how it works as a metaphoric exchanger to construct the human in terms of the mechanical, and the mechanical in terms of the human. Precisely because there was continuing tension between quantification and implication, passages were established between human intelligence and machine behavior. As the rival constellations of homeostasis and reflexivity began to take shape, man and machine were defined in similar terms—as homeostats, or as reflexive devices that threatened to draw the scientists into a morass of subjectivity. Three tropes will illustrate how these processes of metaphoric exchange were mediated by the traffic between concept and artifact. The first crossroads for this material/conceptual traffic is Shannon's electronic rat, a goal-seeking machine that modeled a rat learning a maze. The second is Ross Ashby's homeostat, a device that sought to return to an equilibrium state when disturbed. The third, more an image than a model, envisions a man spliced into an information circuit between two machines. By most standards, for example those invoked by Steve Heims when he questions whether the Macy presentations were good science, the electronic rat and the homeostat were legitimate scientific models. By contrast, the man-in-the-middle image was so loosely defined that it can scarcely qualify as a model at all; moreover, by the time of the Macy conferences it had become a skeuomorph, for automatic devices that replaced the man-in-the-middle had already been used in World War II as early as 1942.[11] Nevertheless, all three tropes func-

10. Heims, *Cybernetics Group* (above, n. 1), p. viii.

11. David B. Parkinson designed a robot gun director for the M-9 antiaircraft gun after having a dream in which he was a member of a Dutch antiaircraft battery that had a marvelous automatic robot gun. The design was implemented in 1942 by Parkinson and two colleagues from Bell Laboratories, Clarence A. Lovell and Bruce T. Weber; it played an important role in the defense of London during World War II. For an account of the gun and a reproduction of Parkinson's original drawing, see the catalogue from the IBM exhibit on the history of the information machine, *A Computer Perspective: A Sequence of 20th-Century Ideas, Events, and Artifacts from the History of the Information Machine,* ed. Glen Fleck (Cambridge, Mass.: Harvard University Press, 1973), pp. 128–129.

tioned as exchangers that brought man and machine into equivalence; all shaped the kinds of stories that participants would tell about what this equivalence meant. In this sense it is irrelevant that some were "good science" and some were not, for they were mutually interactive in establishing the presuppositions of the field. As much as any of the formal theories, these presuppositions defined the shape of the first wave of cybernetics and influenced its direction of flow.

The Electronic Rat, the Homeostat, and the Man-in-the-Middle

There are moments of clarity when the participants in the Macy conferences came close to articulating explicitly the presuppositions informing the deep structure of the discussion. At the seventh conference, John Stroud of the U.S. Naval Electronic Laboratory in San Diego pointed to the far-reaching implications of Shannon's construction of information through the binary distinction between signal and noise. "Mr. Shannon is perfectly justified in being as arbitrary as he wishes," Stroud observed:

> We who listen to him must always keep in mind that he has done so. Nothing that comes out of rigorous argument will be uncontaminated by the particular set of decisions that were made by him at the beginning, and it is rather dangerous at times to generalize. If we at any time relax our awareness of the way in which we originally defined the signal, we thereby automatically call all of the remainder of the received message the "not" signal or noise.[12]

As Stroud realized, Shannon's distinction between signal and noise had a conservative bias that privileges stasis over change. Noise interferes with the exact replication of the message, which is presumed to be the desired result. The structure of the theory implied that change was deviation, and that deviation should be corrected. By contrast, MacKay's theory had as its generative distinction the difference in the state of the receiver's mind before and after the message arrived. In his model, information was not *opposed* to change, it *was* change.

Applied to goal-seeking behavior, the two theories pointed in different directions. Privileging signal over noise, Shannon's theory implied that the goal was a preexisting state toward which the mechanism would move by making a series of distinctions between correct and incorrect choices. The goal was stable, and the mechanism would achieve stability when it reached the goal. This con-

12. *Cybernetics* (Seventh Conference, 1951), p. 155.

struction easily led to the implication that the goal, formulated in general and abstract terms, was less a specific site than stability itself. Thus the construction of information as a signal/noise distinction and the privileging of homeostasis produced and were produced by each other. By contrast, MacKay's theory implied that the goal was not a fixed point but a constantly evolving dance between expectation and surprise. In his model, setting a goal temporarily marked a state that itself would become enfolded into a reflexive spiral of change. In Gregory Bateson's phrase, information was a difference that made a difference. In the same way that signal/ noise and homeostasis went together, so did reflexivity and information as a signifying difference.

These correlations imply that before Shannon's electronic rat ever set marker in maze, it was constituted through assumptions that affected how it would be interpreted. Although Shannon called his device a maze-solving machine, the Macy group quickly dubbed it a rat.[13] The machine consisted of a 5×5 square grid, through which a sensing finger moved. An electric jack that could be plugged into any of the 25 squares marked the goal, and the machine's task was to move through the squares by orderly search procedures until it reached the jack. The machine could remember previous search patterns and either repeat them or not, depending on whether they had been successful. While Heinz von Foerster, Margaret Mead, and Hans Teuber in their introduction to the eighth conference volume highlighted the electronic rat's significance, they also acknowledged its limitations: "We all know that we ought to study the organism, and not the computers, if we wish to understand the organism. Differences in levels of organization may be more than quantitative."[14] They went on to argue, however, that "the computing robot provides us with analogues that are helpful as far as they seem to hold, and no less helpful whenever they break down. To find out in what ways a nervous system (or a social group) differs from our man-made analogues requires experiment. These experiments would not have been considered if the analogue had not been proposed."[15]

There is another way to understand this linkage. By suggesting certain kinds of experiments, the analogues between intelligent machines and humans *construct the human in terms of the machine.*

13. Claude E. Shannon, "Presentation of a Maze-Solving Machine," *Cybernetics* (Eighth Conference, 1952), pp. 173–180.

14. *Cybernetics* (Eighth Conference, 1952), p. xix.

15. Ibid.

Even when the experiment fails, the basic terms of the comparison operate to constitute the signifying difference. If I say a chicken is not like a tractor, I have characterized the chicken in terms of the tractor, no less than when I assert that the two are alike. In the same way, whether it is understood as like or unlike, human intelligence ranged alongside an intelligent machine is put into a relay system that constitutes the human as a special kind of information machine, and the information machine as a special kind of human. Moreover, although some characteristics of the analogy may be explicitly denied, the presuppositions it embodies cannot be denied, for they are intrinsic to being able to think the model. The presuppositions embodied in the electronic rat include the idea that both humans and cybernetic machines are goal-seeking mechanisms learning through corrective feedback to reach a stable state. Both are information processors that tend toward homeostasis when they are functioning correctly.

Given these assumptions, it is perhaps predictable that reflexivity should be constructed in this model as neurosis. Shannon, demonstrating how his electronic rat could get caught in a reflexive loop that would keep it circling endlessly around, remarked that "it has established a vicious circle, or a singing condition."[16] "Singing condition" is a phrase that Warren McCulloch and Warren Pitts had used in an earlier presentation to describe neuroses modeled through cybernetic neural nets. If machines are like humans in having neuroses, humans are like machines in having neuroses that can be modeled mechanically. Linking humans and machines in a common circuit, the analogy constructs both as equilibrium systems that become pathological when they fall into reflexivity. This kind of mutually constitutive interaction belies the implication in the volume's introduction that such analogues are neutral heuristic devices. More accurately, they are relay systems that transport assumptions from one arena to the next. Some of these assumptions may be explicitly recognized and in this sense authorized; others are not. Whether authorized or unauthorized, they are part of the context that guides inquiry, suggests models, and intimates conclusions.

The assumptions traveling across the relay system set up by homeostasis are perhaps most visible in the discussion of W. Ross Ashby's homeostat.[17] The homeostat was an electrical device con-

16. Ibid., p. 173.

17. W. Ross Ashby, "Homeostasis," in *Cybernetics* (Ninth Conference, 1953), pp. 73–108.

structed with transducers and variable resistors. When it received an input changing its state, it searched for the configuration of variables that would return it to its initial condition. Ashby explained that the homeostat was meant to model an organism that must keep essential variables within preset limits in order to survive. He emphasized that the cost of exceeding those limits is death: if homeostasis equals safety ("Your life would be safe," Ashby responded, when demonstrating how the machine could return to homeostasis[18]), departure from homeostasis threatens death. It is not difficult to discern in this rhetoric of danger and safety echoes of the traumatic experiences of World War II. One of Ashby's examples, for instance, concerns an engineer sitting at the control panel of a ship: the engineer functions like a homeostat as he strives to keep the dials within certain limits to prevent catastrophe. Human and machine are alike in needing stable interior environments. The human keeps the ship's interior stable, and this stability preserves the homeostasis of the human's interior, which in its turn allows the human to continue to ensure the ship's homeostasis. Arguing that homeostasis is a requirement "uniform among the inanimate and the animate," Ashby privileged it as a universally desirable state.[19]

The postwar context for the Macy conferences played an important role in formulating what counted as homeostasis. Given the cataclysm of the war, it seemed self-evident that homeostasis was meaningful only if it included the environment as part of the picture. Thus Ashby conceived of the homeostat as a device that included both the organism and the environment. "Our question is how the organism is going to struggle with its environment," he remarked, "and if that question is to be treated adequately, we must assume some specific environment."[20] This specificity was expressed through the homeostat's four units, which could be arranged in various configurations to simulate organism-plus-environment. For example, one unit could be designated "organism" and the remaining three the "environment"; in another arrangement, three of the units might be the "organism," with the remaining one the "environment." Formulated in general terms, the problem the homeostat addressed was this: Given some function of the environment E, can the organism find an inverse function E^{-1} such that the product of the two will result in an equilibrium state?

18. Ibid., p. 79.

19. Ibid., p. 73.

20. Ibid., pp. 73–74.

When Ashby asked Macy participants whether such a solution could be found for highly nonlinear systems, Julian H. Bigelow correctly answered "In general, no."[21] Yet, as Walter Pitts observed, the fact that an organism continues to live means that a solution does exist. More precisely, the problem was whether a solution could be articulated within the mathematical conventions and technologies of representation available to express it. These limits, in turn, were constituted through the specificities of the model that translated between the question in the abstract and the particular question posed by that experiment. Thus the emphasis shifted from finding a solution to stating the problem.

This dynamic appears repeatedly through the Macy discussions. Participants increasingly understood the ability to specify exactly what was wanted as the limiting factor for building machines that could perform human functions. At the ninth conference, Walter Pitts was confident enough of the construction to claim it as accepted knowledge: "At the very beginning of these meetings, the question was frequently under discussion of whether a machine could be built which would do a particular thing, and, of course, the answer, which everybody has realized by now, is that as long as you definitely specify what you want the machine to do, you can, in principle, build a machine to do it."[22] If what is exactly stated can be done by a machine, the residue of the uniquely human becomes coextensive with the qualities of language that interfere with precise specification—its ambiguity, metaphoric play, multiple encoding, and allusive exchanges between one symbol system and another. The uniqueness of human behavior thus becomes assimilated to the ineffability of language, while the common ground that humans and machines share is identified with the univocality of an instrumental language that has banished ambiguity from its lexicon. This train of thought indicates how the rival constellations of homeostasis and reflexivity assimilated other elements into themselves. On the side of homeostasis was instrumental language, while ambiguity, allusion, and metaphor stood with reflexivity.

By today's standards Ashby's homeostat was a simple machine, but it had encoded within it a complex network of assumptions. Paradoxically, the model's simplicity facilitated rather than hampered the overlay of assumptions onto the artifact, for its very lack of complicating detail meant that the model stood for much more than it physically enacted. Ashby acknowledged during discussion

21. Ibid., p. 75.

22. Ibid., p. 107.

that the homeostat was a simple model and asserted that he "would like to get on to the more difficult case of the clever animal that has a lot of nervous system and is, nevertheless, trying to get itself stable."[23] The slippage between the simplicity of the model and the complexity of the phenomena did not go unremarked. J. Z. Young, from the anatomy department at University College London, sharply responded, "Actually that is experimentally rather dangerous. You are all talking about the cortex and you have it very much in mind. Simpler systems have only a limited number of possibilities."[24] Yet the "simpler systems" helped to reinforce the idea that humans are mechanisms that respond to their environments by trying to maintain homeostasis; that the function of scientific language is exact specification; that the bottleneck for creating intelligent machines lay in formulating problems exactly; and that a concept of information that privileges exactness over meaning is therefore more suitable to model construction than one that does not. Ashby's homeostat, Shannon's information theory, and the electronic rat were collaborators in constructing an interconnected network of assumptions about language, teleology, and human behavior.

These assumptions did not go uncontested. The concept that most clearly brought them into question was reflexivity. Appropriately, the borderland where reflexivity contested the claims of homeostasis was the man-in-the-middle. The image was introduced in the sixth conference in John Stroud's analysis of an operator sandwiched between a radar tracking device on one side and an antiaircraft gun on the other. The gun operator, Stroud observed, is "surrounded on both sides by very precisely known mechanisms and the question comes up, 'What kind of a machine have we put in the middle.'"[25] The image as Stroud used it constructs the man as an input/output device: information comes in from the radar, travels through the man, and goes out through the gun. The man is significantly placed in the *middle* of the circuit, where his output and input are already spliced into an existing loop. Were he at the end, it might be necessary to consider more complex factors, such as how he was interacting with an open-ended evironment whose state could not be exactly specified and whose future evolution was unknown. The focus in Stroud's presentation was on how informa-

23. Ibid., p. 97.

24. Ibid., p.100.

25. John Stroud, "The Psychological Moment in Perception," in *Cybernetics* (Sixth Conference, 1949), pp. 27–63, esp. pp. 27–28.

tion is transformed as it moves through the man-in-the-middle. As with the electronic rat and the homeostat, the emphasis was on predictability and homeostatic stability.

Countering this view was Frank Fremont-Smith's recognition of the inescapable reflexivity inherent in constructing this system as a system. "Probably man is never only between the two machines," Fremont-Smith pointed out. "Certainly he is never only in between two machines when you are studying him because you are the other man who is making an input into the man. You are studying and changing his relation to the machines by virtue of the fact that you are studying him."[26] Fremont-Smith's opening of the circuit to the environment through reflexivity was later countered by Stroud in a revealing image that sought once again to close the circuit: "The human being is the most marvelous set of instruments," he observed, "but like all portable instrument sets the human observer is noisy and erratic in operation. However, if these are all the instruments you have, you have to work with them until something better comes along."[27] In Stroud's remark, the open-endedness of Fremont-Smith's construction is converted into a portable instrument set. The instrument may not be physically connected to two mechanistic terminals, the image implied, but this lack of tight connection only makes the splice invisible. It does not negate the suture that constructs the human as an information-processing machine that ideally should be homeostatic in its operation, however noisy it is in practice.

As his switch to formal address indicates, Fremont-Smith was apparently upset at the recuperation of his comment back into the presuppositions of homeostasis. "You cannot possibly, Dr. Stroud, eliminate the human being. Therefore what I am saying and trying to emphasize is that, with all their limitations, it might be pertinent for those scientific investigators at the general level, who find to their horror that we have to work with human beings, to make as much use as possible of the insights available as to what human beings are like and how they operate."[28] His comment cuts to the heart of the objection against reflexivity. Whether construed as "subjective information" or as changes in the observer's representations, reflexivity opens the man-in-the-middle to internal psychological complexity so that he can no longer be constructed as a black box functioning as an input/output device. The fear is that

26. *Cybernetics* (Sixth Conference, 1949), p. 147.

27. Ibid., p. 153.

28. Ibid.

under these conditions, reliable quantification becomes elusive or impossible and science slips into subjectivity, which to many conferees meant that it was not real science at all. Confirming traditional ideas of how science should be done in a postwar atmosphere that was already clouded by the hysteria of McCarthyism, homeostasis thus implied a return to normalcy in more than one sense.

The thrust of Fremont-Smith's observations was, of course, to intimate that psychological complexity was unavoidable. The responses of other participants reveal that it was precisely this implication they were most concerned to deny. Were their responses valid objections, or themselves evidence of the very subconscious resistance they were trying to disavow? The primary spoksperson for this latter disconcerting possibility was Lawrence Kubie, a psychoanalyst from the Yale University Psychiatric Clinic. In correspondence, Kubie enraged other participants by interpreting their comments as evidence of their psychological states rather than as matters for scientific debate. In his presentations he was more tactful, but the reflexive thrust of his argument remained clear. His presentations occupy more space in the published transcripts than those of any other participant, comprising about one-sixth of the total. Although he met with repeated skepticism among the physical scientists, he continued to try to explain and defend his position. At the center of his explanation was the multiply encoded nature of language, operating at once as an instrument that the speaker could use to communicate and as a reflexive mirror that revealed more than the speaker knew. Like MacKay's theory of information, Kubie's psychoanalytic approach built reflexivity into the model. Also like MacKay's theory, the greatest conscious resistance it met was the demand for reliable quantification.

Kubie's presentations grew increasingly entrenched as the conferences proceeded. The resistance they generated illustrates why reflexivity had to be redefined if it was to be rescued from the dead end to which, in the view of many participants, it seemed to lead. From the point of view of those who resisted Kubie's ideas, psychoanalysis collapsed the distance between speaker and language, turning what should be objective scientific debate into a tar baby that clung to them more closely the more they tried to push it away. The association of reflexivity with psychoanalysis probably delivered the death blow to the reflexivity constellation. Homeostasis seemed to have won the day. Ironically, however, its triumph was also its senescence, for, divorced from the reflexivity constellation, it lost its power to generate new ideas and to serve as an impetus for further research. After about 1960, homeostasis became a skeuo-morph, pointing back to an earlier period but also serving as a link to a more radical form of reflexivity. To be acceptable to the community that grew out of the Macy conferences, a mode of reflexivity had to be devised that could be contained within stable boundaries and divorced from the feedback loop that implicated the observer in everything he said. Maturana's epistemology of autopoiesis satisfied these conditions in one sense, although, as we shall see, in another sense it profoundly subverted them.

Autopoiesis and the Closure of the System

Maturana's epistemology is grounded in work he did in the late 1950s and early 1960s on visual processing in the frog's cortex. He coauthored the influential paper "What the Frog's Eye Tells the Frog's Brain," which demonstrated that the frog's visual cortex responds to stimuli in ways specific to the species.[29] The frog's brain discussed in this article, far from being a "natural" object, is as much an artifact as the electronic rat and the homeostat. To make the brain productive of scientific knowledge, precisely placed microelectrodes were inserted into it using stereotactic surgical equipment; the electrodes were then connected to complex electronic monitoring systems. Spliced into a circuit that included the experimenter's observations as well as the laboratory equipment, the frog brain (I drop the possessive because at this point the brain no longer belonged strictly to the frog) became a techno-bioapparatus instantiating the cybernetic framework that constituted animals and machines as information-processing systems, even as it was used to advance and develop that same framework.

Thus reflexively constructed, the frog brain showed little response to large slow-moving objects, while small quickly-moving objects evoked a large response. The response pattern is obviously adaptive for frogs, since it enables them to detect flies and other prey while screening out other phenomena that might distract them. The radical implication of this work is summarized in the authors' conclusion that "the [frog's] eye speaks to the brain in a language already highly processed and interpreted."[30] Imaginatively giving the frog brain back to the frog, I have elsewhere tried to envision what Newton's three laws of motion might look like to a

29. J. Y. Lettvin, H. R. Maturana, W. S. McCulloch, and W. H. Pitts, "What the Frog's Eye Tells the Frog's Brain," *Proceedings of the Institute of Radio Engineers* 47: 11 (1959): 1940–1959.

30. Ibid., p. 1950.

frog. The commonsense observation that an object at rest remains the same object when it is in motion would be scarcely conceivable from a frog's point of view, for the two kinds of objects are processed in completely different ways by the frog's sensory system. The point is not, of course, that humans can see more or better than frogs. Rather, if perception is species-specific, then it follows that every perception is always already encoded by the perceptual apparatus of the observer, whether the observer is a human or a frog. Thus there is no possibility of a transcendent position from which to see reality as it "really" is. Simply put, the article blows a frog-sized hole in objectivist epistemology.

Despite its radical implications, the article's *form* is in the mainstream of scientific tradition, for nothing in the way it is written challenges scientific objectivity. Nowhere do the authors acknowledge that their observations are made from a human perspective and thus are relative to the perceptual apparatus of the human sensorium. Later work by Maturana made this inconsistency even more apparent, for it questioned whether the [primate] brain creates a "representation" of the outside world at all.[31] Data from the techno-bioapparatus of the primate visual cortex demonstrated that there is no qualitative correspondence between stimulus and response, and only a small quantitative correspondence. Maturana thus concluded that the stimulus acts as a trigger for a response dictated almost entirely by the internal organization of the frog sensory receptors and central nervous system. But here language betrays me, for if what happens inside the frog cortex is not a representation of what happens outside, then it is misleading to talk about stimulus and response, for such language implies a one-to-one correlation between the two events. What is needed, evidently, is another kind of language that would do justice to Maturana's revolutionary insight that "there is no observation without an observer."

To solve the problem, Maturana proposed a radical new epistemology that rejected traditional causality. So powerful is this epistemology that it can rightfully be considered to create a different kind of world, which I will attribute to Maturana (thus ironically restoring to his name the possessive that had earlier been taken from the frog's brain when it became a site for scientific knowledge production). In Maturana's world, one event does not cause anoth-

31. H. R. Maturana, G. Uribe, and S. Frenk, "A Biological Theory of Relativistic Color Coding in the Primate Retina," *Archivos de biologia y medicina experimentales*, suppl. 1 (Santiago, Chile: 1969).

er—rather, events act as "triggers" for responses determined by a system's self-organization. Maturana defined a self-organizing system as a composite unity: it is a unity because it has a coherent organization, and it is composite because it consists of components whose relations with each other and with other systems constitute the organization that defines the system as such. Thus the components constitute the system, and the system unites the components. The circularity of the reasoning foregrounds reflexivity while also transforming it. Whereas in the Macy conferences reflexivity was associated with psychological complexity, in Maturana's world it is constituted through the interplay between a system and its components. They mutually define each other in the bootstrap operation characteristic of reflexive self-constitution.

Reflexivity is also central to the distinction Maturana makes between allopoietic and autopoietic systems. Allopoietic systems have as their goal something exterior to themselves. When I use my car to drive to work, I am using it as an allopoietic system, for its function is transportation, a goal exterior to the maintenance of its internal organization. As the example indicates, allopoietic systems are defined functionally and teleologically rather than reflexively. By contrast, autopoietic systems have as their goal the maintenance of their own organization. If my foremost purpose in life is to continue living, then I am functioning as an autopoietic system, for I have as my goal the maintenance of my self-organization. One can see in this formulation the ghost of homeostasis, although it now signifies not so much stability as a formal closure of the system upon itself.

Maturana's world was developed in part as a reaction against behaviorism. Von Foerster, who worked with him on a number of projects, anticipated Maturana's rejection of behaviorism when he contested the behaviorist account of a conditioned subject as a "black box" that gives a predictable output for a known input (a scenario reminiscent of what Stroud wanted to do with the man-in-the-middle). Von Foerster turned behaviorism on its head by shifting the focus to the experimenter-observer. He argued that behaviorist experiments do not prove that living creatures are black boxes; rather, they demonstrate that the experimenter has simplified his environment so it has become predictable, while perserving intact his own complexity and free will.[32] In Maturana's terms, the experimenter has converted the experimental subject into an al-

32. Heinz von Foerster, "Molecular Ethology: An Immodest Proposal for Semantic Clarification," in *Observing Systems* (above, n. 2), pp. 150–188.

lopoietic system, while continuing to function himself as an autopoietic system. The critique gives a political edge to Maturana's
epistemology, for it points to the power relations that determine
who gets to function autopoietically and who is reduced to al-
lopoiesis. Applying von Foerster's arguments to Maturana's experimental work leads to the ironic conclusion that the frog brain was
made into an allopoietic system so that it could buttress arguments
for the importance of autopoiesis.

The reasoning illustrates the difficulty of working out the implications of a reflexive epistemology, for the ground keeps shifting
depending on which viewpoint is adopted (for example, that of the
frog versus that of the experimenter). Maturana was able to carry
his conclusions as far as he did because he displaced the focus of attention from the boundary between a system and the environment, to the feedback loops within the organism. The price he pays
for the valuable insights this move yields is the erasure of the environment. In Maturana's world, the environment becomes a nebu-
lous "medium" populated by self-organizing systems that interact
with each other through their structural couplings with the medium. Resisting the closure into black boxes that the reductive causality of behaviorism would effect, Maturana performs another kind
of closure that can give only a weak account of how systems interact with their environment and with each other. If reflexivity is finally given its due, it is at the price of giving a full and rich account of interactivity.

In the third wave of cybernetics, the self-organization that is a
central feature of Maturana's world lingers on as a skeuomorph,
and the emphasis shifts to emergence and immersion. Whereas for
Maturana self-organization was associated with homeostasis, in the
simulated computer worlds of the third wave, self-organization is
seen as the engine driving systems toward emergence. Interest is fo-
cused not on how systems maintain their organization intact, but
rather on how they evolve in unpredictable and often highly complex ways through emergent processes. Although I take these simulated worlds to include artificial life as well as virtual reality, in the
interest of space I will discuss only the latter, and that briefly. How
does the history of overlapping innovation and replication, of
skeuomorphs connecting one era with another, and of traffic
through such artifacts as the homeostat, the electronic rat, and the
frog cortex, matter to the development of virtual reality? What
webbed network of connections mediate cybernetics for virtual reality technologies, and what issues are foregrounded by exploring
these connections?

The Sedimented History of Virtual Reality

Cybernetics is connected to virtual reality technologies in much the same way as Cartesian space is connected to contemporary mapmaking. Through such seminal ideas as information, feedback loops, human-machine interfaces, and circular causality, cybernetics provided the terminology and conceptual framework that made virtual reality a possibility, although the pathways between any given cybernetic theory and virtual reality technology may be indirect and highly mediated. From this tangled web, I will pull three strands that I think have important consequences for VR: embodiment, reflexivity, and positionality. The first thread is spun from Claude Shannon's move of conceptualizing information as a pattern distinct from the physical markers that embody it. As we have seen, this move allowed information to be reliably quantified. It also created a way of thinking about information that made it seem disembodied, removed from the material substrate in which it is instantiated. This construction of information allows cyberspace to be conceptualized as a disembodied realm of information that humans enter by leaving their bodies behind. In this realm, so the story goes, we are transformed into information ourselves and thus freed from the constraints of embodiment. We can take whatever form we wish, including no form at all.

In fact, of course, we are never disembodied. Simulated worlds can exist for us only because we can perceive them through the techno-bioapparatus of our body spliced into the cybernetic circuit. The reading of cyberspace as a disembodied realm is a skeuomorph that harks back to the first wave of cybernetics, which in turn is a reading of information that reinscribes into cybernetics a very old and traditional distinction between form and matter. These residues, echoing in a chain of allusion and reinscription that stretches back to Plato's cave, testify to the importance of excavating the sedimented history of artifacts and concepts, for they allow us to understand how the inertial weight of tradition continues to exert gravitational pull on the present.

Although the perception that cyberspace is disembodied is refuted by the material realities of the situation, it nevertheless has a material effect on what technologies will be developed, how they will be used, and what kind of virtual worlds they will instantiate. If the point is to enhance perceptions of disembodiment, then the technology will insulate the users as much as possible from their immediate surroundings. Rather than develop open systems such as Mandala that emphasize the user's connection to the environment, the industry will continue to push head-mounted displays and stereo eyephones that cut the users off from their surroundings in the real world. If, on the contrary, the link between the virtual experience and embodiment is perceived to be important, then simulations such as *Placeholder* will be developed.[33] Designed by Brenda Laurel and Rachel Strickland, *Placeholder* requires the user to choose one of four totemic animals in which to be embodied. If the user chooses Crow, she negotiates the virtual terrain by flying; if Snake, her vision shifts to infrared and she moves by crawling. Obviously this is not a reinscription of the "natural" body in the virtual world, since these experiences are not normally available to the human sensorium. Rather, the simulation recognizes that the virtual body is a techno-bioapparatus, but in a way that emphasizes rather than conceals the centrality of embodiment to experience.

The next thread I want to pull from the skein is reflexivity. The struggle to introduce reflexivity into cybernetics makes clear how difficult it is to include the observer in the situation and to realize fully the implications of this inclusion. Virtual reality technologies can facilitate this realization, for by providing a prosthesis to the "natural" sensorium, they make the experience of mediated perception immediately obvious to the user. Structural coupling, Maturana's phrase for how self-organizing systems interact with each other and the surrounding medium, seems a cumbersome, roundabout way to say something simple like "I see the dog" if one is speaking from the position of the "natural" body. If the dog appears in a VR simulation, however, then it becomes common sense to realize that one "sees" the dog only through the structural couplings that put one's visual cortex in a feedback loop with the simulated image. These couplings include the interfaces between the retina and the stereovision helmet, between the helmet and the computer through data transmission cables, between the incoming data and the CTR display via computer algorithms, and between the algorithms and silicon chips through the magnetic polarities recorded on the chips. In this sense VR technologies instantiate Maturana's world, converting what may seem like abstract and far-out ideas into experiential realities.

Taken to the extreme, the awareness of the mediated nature of

33. Brenda Laurel and Rachel Strickland showed a video about *Placeholder* at the Fourth International Cyberconference at Banff Centre for the Arts in May 1994. The simulation is so complex that it requires ten computers to run it, including two Onyx Reality Machines; it will probably never be shown publically for this reason, much less marketed. It demonstrates how far the industry still is from creating a multiperson, interactive simulation that takes embodiment fully into account.

perception that VR technologies provide can be taken to signify that the body itself is a prosthesis.[34] The only difference between the body and VR couplings, in this view, is that the body was acquired before birth through organic means rather than purchased from some high-tech VR laboratory like VPL. The body, like the VR body-suit, creates mediated perceptions; both operate through structural couplings with the environment. In this account we can see the thread of disembodiment getting entangled with the thread of reflexivity, creating a view of the subject that sees human embodiment as one option among many, neither more nor less artificial than the VR prostheses that extend perception into simulated worlds. Is it necessary to insist, once again, that embodiment is not an option but a necessity in order for life to exist? The account elides the complex structures that have evolved through millennia in coadaptive processes that have fitted us as organisms to our environment. Compared to the complexity and depth of this adaptation, the VR body-suit is a wrinkle in the fabric of human life, hardly to be mistaken as an alternative form of embodiment. Knowing the history of cybernetics can be helpful in maintaining a sense of scale, for the move of mapping complex assumptions onto relatively simple artifacts has occurred before, usually in the service of eliding the immense differences between the complexities of the human organism and the comparatively simple architectures of the machines.

The last thread I want to unravel concerns the position of the VR user. I take "positionality" to include the body in which the user is incarnate, the language she speaks, and the culture in which she is immersed, as well as the specificities and collectivities of her individual history—but the part of positionality that concerns me here is her relation to the technology. The narrative of cybernetics as I have constructed it here suggests that the field is moving along a trajectory that arcs from homeostasis to reflexivity to emergence/immersion. First stability is privileged; then a system's ability to take as its goal the maintenance of its own organization; then its ability to manifest emergent and unpredictable properties. Inscribing the human subject into this trajectory, we can say that in the first stage, the privileged goal is for the human to remain an autonomous and homeostatic subject; in the second stage, to change structurally but nevertheless to maintain her internal organization

34. See, for example, Mark Pesce's presentation at the Third International Cyberconference in Austin, Texas, May 1993, entitled "Final Amputation: Pathologic Ontology in Cyberspace" (forthcoming in the electronic journal *Speed*).

intact; and in the third stage, to mutate into a new kind of form through emergent processes that evolve spontaneously through feedback loops between human and machine.

The larger narrative inscribed here thus locates the subject in a changing relation to intelligent machines that points toward a looming transformation: the era of the human is about to give way, or has already given way, to the posthuman. There are already in circulation various accounts of how this transformation will come about and what it will mean. Howard Rheingold has called it IA, intelligence augmentation, arguing that humans and intelligent machines are entering into a symbiosis to which each will bring the talents and gifts specific to their species: humans will contribute to the partnership pattern recognition, language capability, and understanding ambiguities; machines will contribute rapid calculation, massive memory storage, and rapid data retrieval.[35] Bruce Mazlish has called the posthuman era the fourth discontinuity, arguing that it constitutes the latest of four decisive breaks in human subjectivity.[36] Hans Moravec sees the break more pessimistically, arguing that protein-based life forms are about to be superseded by silicon-based life and that humans will soon become obsolete.[37] The differences between these accounts notwithstanding, they concur in seeing the posthuman era as constituting a decisive break in the history of humankind. The narrative offered here aims to counter this apocalyptic tone of sudden and irreversible change by looking closely at how change has actually occurred in the history of cybernetics. Concepts and artifacts are never invented out of whole cloth; rather, they embody a sedimented history that exerts an inertial pull on the new even as it modifies the old. If it is true that we are on the threshold of becoming posthuman, surely it behooves us to understand the overlapping patterns of replication and innovation that have brought us to where we now are.

35. Howard Rheingold, *Virtual Reality* (New York: Summit Books, 1991).

36. Bruce Mazlish, *The Fourth Discontinuity: The Co-Evolution of Humans and Machines* (New Haven: Yale University Press, 1993).

37. Moravec, *Mind Children* (above, n. 5), pp. 1–5.

What Is an Electronic Author?

Theory and the

Technological Fallacy

Richard Grusin

At the end of his now-classic essay "What Is an Author?" Michel
Foucault writes: "The author—or what I have called the 'author-
function'—is undoubtedly only one of the possible specifications of
the subject and, considering past historical transformations, it appears that the form, the complexity, and even the existence of this
function are far from immutable. We can easily imagine a culture
where discourse would circulate without any need for an author."[1]
Foucault's essay has most often been read as proclaiming the much-
celebrated "death of the author." In posing the question of electronic authorship, I take up one particular version of the death-of-
the-author story, the increasingly fashionable tale that the
technologies of electronic writing have brought us to the verge (if
not into the very midst) of this imaginary culture "where discourse
would circulate without any need for an author." By examining the
critical discourse in which the theory and practice of electronic
writing are being articulated, I want to single out the discursive logic that structures the current articulation of electronic authorship. I
focus mainly on four of the most important recent books on electronic writing: Mark Poster, *The Mode of Information*; Jay Bolter,
Writing Space; George Landow, *Hypertext*; and Richard Lanham, *The*

---

1. Michel Foucault, "What Is an Author?" in *Language, Counter-Memory, Practice: Selected Essays and Interviews by Michel Foucault*, ed. Donald F. Bouchard, trans. Donald F.
Bouchard and Sherry Simon (Ithaca, N.Y.: Cornell University Press, 1977), p. 138.

39

Electronic Word—all but the first of which have appeared both in print and in electronic formats.[2]

Given the limited aims of this essay, however, I do not undertake an analysis of the electronic versions of these texts. Rather, I articulate the logic of authorship that emerges from these works as emblematic of the contemporary discourse of electronic writing—a discursive logic that frequently takes the form of a kind of technological determinism, which we might best characterize (with a nod toward Wimsatt and Beardsley) as constituting a technological fallacy. This fallacy most often manifests itself in propositional statements that ascribe agency to technology itself, statements in which the technologies of electronic writing are described as actors. For example:

> The electronic word democratizes the world of arts and letters.[3]

> Pixeled print calls this basic stylistic decorum [the best style is the style not noticed], and the social ideal built upon it, into question.[4]

> The computer rewrites the history of writing by sending us back to reconsider nearly every aspect of the earlier technologies.[5]

> [E]lectronic texts naturally join themselves into larger and larger structures, into encyclopedias and libraries.[6]

> Electronic writing . . . disperses the subject so that it no longer functions as a center in the way it did in pre-electronic writing.[7]

> Computer writing, instantaneously available over the globe, inserts itself into a non-linear temporality that unsettles the relation to the writing subject.[8]

2. Mark Poster, *The Mode of Information: Poststructuralism and Social Context* (Chicago: University of Chicago Press, 1990); J. David Bolter, *Writing Space: The Computer in the History of Literacy* (Hillsdale, N.J.: Lawrence Erlbaum, 1990); George Landow, *Hypertext: The Convergence of Contemporary Critical Thoery and Technology* (Baltimore: Johns Hopkins University Press, 1992); Richard Lanham, *The Electronic Word: Democracy, Technology, and the Arts* (Chicago: University of Chicago Press, 1993).

3. Lanham, *Electronic Word*, p. 23.

4. Ibid., p. 4.

5. Bolter, *Writing Space*, p. 46.

6. Ibid., p. 89.

7. Poster, *Mode of Information*, p. 100.

8. Ibid., p. 128.

[H]ypermedia linking automatically produces collaboration.[9]

Hypertext systems, just like printed books, dramatically change the roles of student, teacher, assignment, evaluation, reading list, as well as relations among individual instructors, courses, departments, and disciplines.[10]

In calling attention to these formulations I do not mean to suggest that they are in any way unique. Indeed, it is precisely the unremarkability of such propositions that I mean to remark. The fact that any number of similar sentences could have been drawn from these or other recent works on electronic writing attests to the powerful discursive logic that these works exemplify in thinking about the relation between electronic technologies and the theory and practice of authorship, a logic that I start to articulate in this essay. My argument has three parts. I begin with a discussion of the idea that the new electronic technologies realize or instantiate the theoretical assertions of poststructuralism, postmodernism, or deconstruction. I next look at some of the ways in which claims for the agency of electronic technologies in changing cultural practice often elide or marginalize the materiality of these technologies. Finally, I conclude with some speculations about why the discursive logic of electronic authorship tends consistently to represent new technologies as the primary, if not the sole, agents of fundamental change, and some suggestions about the direction that future discussions of electronic authorship might best take.

Although differing on the precise details of the relation between theory, technology, and culture, all four authors would probably assent to Lanham's contention that "it is hard not to think that, at the end of the day, electronic text will seem the natural fulfillment of much current literary theory, and resolve many of its questions."[11] In fact the title of one of Lanham's chapters—"The Extraordinary Convergence: Democracy, Technology, Theory, and the University Curriculum"—itself converges with one of the central theses of Landow's book, set forth fairly explicitly in its subtitle: *The Convergence of Contemporary Critical Theory and Technology*.[12] Thus, even while Landow begins his book by endorsing J. Hillis

9. Landow, *Hypertext*, p. 95.

10. Ibid., p. 163.

11. Lanham, *Electronic Word*, p. 130.

12. Ibid., p. 101.

Miller's contention that the relation "between electronic comput-ing, hypertext in particular, and literary theory of the past three or four decades" is "'multiple, non-linear, non-causal, non-dialectical, and heavily overdetermined,'" he most often describes this rela-tionship as taking the form of electronic technologies converging with or embodying the claims of poststructural theory.[13] "[H]yper-text," Landow writes, "embodies many of the ideas and attitudes proposed by Barthes, Derrida, Foucault, and others."[14] This is par-ticularly true, he argues, of Derrida, who "more than almost any other contemporary theorist . . . uses the terms *link, web, network, matrix,* and *interweaving,* associated with hypertextuality."[15] Else-where in the book Landow describes grammatology as "the art and science of hypertext."[16] He characterizes hypertext as "imple-ment[ing] Derrida's call for a new form of hieroglyphic writing that can avoid some of the problems implicit and therefore inevitable in Western writing systems and their printed versions,"[17] as well as touting hypertext as the "embodi[ment] of the Derridean text."[18] Hypertext, which Landow defines as "the convergence of poststruc-turalist conceptions of textuality and electronic embodiments of it," is seen to reconfigure the electronic author in two basic ways: by breaking down the distinction between author and reader, and by constituting the self of author and reader alike as "a de-centered (or centerless) network of codes that, on another level, also serves as a node within another centerless network."[19]

Like Lanham and Landow, Bolter and Poster also see the tech-nologies of electronic writing as reconfiguring the authorial self. But where Landow in particular sees electronic writing as realizing or instantiating deconstructive accounts of the relations among au-thors, texts, and meanings, Bolter and Poster see these relations as more problematic. Building on the work of (among others) Walter Ong, Bolter sees electronic writing as signaling our location at the end of the late age of print. For Bolter, "electronic writing empha-sizes the impermanence and changeability of text, and it tends to reduce the distance between author and reader by turning the read-

13. Landow, *Hypertext,* p. 27.

14. Ibid., p. 73.

15. Ibid., p. 25.

16. Ibid., p. 30.

17. Ibid., p. 43.

18. Ibid., p. 59.

19. Ibid., p. 73.

er into an author. The computer is restructuring our current economy of writing. It is changing the cultural status of writing as well as the method of producing books. It is changing the relationship of the author to the text and of both author and text to the reader."[20] In Bolter's formulation, agency is ascribed primarily to the computer: electronic information technology is the agent that dictates or determines change.

Like Landow, Bolter represents the effects of the computer as resembling poststructuralist claims about writing; he notices, for example, the way in which "even the most radical theorists (Barthes, de Man, Derrida, and their American followers) speak a language that is strikingly appropriate to electronic writing."[21] "Derrida's characterization of a text," he writes, "sounds very much like text in the electronic writing space."[22] Despite the affinities between poststructuralist theory and electronic writing, however, Bolter remains convinced that computer technology is the agent of a fundamental change in the nature of writing, a change that, because deconstruction cannot finally be sufficient to it, will require the development of a new theory of writing. "Electronic writing takes us beyond the paradox of deconstruction, because it accepts as strengths the very qualities—the play of signs, intertextuality, the lack of closure—that deconstruction poses as the ultimate limitations of literature and language."[23] Although "deconstruction has helped to free us from a mode of thought that was too closely wedded to the technology of print," Bolter concludes, it is not a theory of electronic writing. Deconstruction can only tell us "what electronic writing is not. We will still need a new literary theory to achieve a positive understanding of electronic writing."[24]

One attempt at such a new theory is offered by Poster, who hybridizes Marx, McLuhan, and Baudrillard in formulating the concept of the "mode of information," which functions for him as a periodizing concept analogous to Marx's mode of production.

> Every age employs forms of symbolic exchange which contain internal and external structures, means and relations of signification. Stages in the mode of information may be tentatively designated as follows: face-to-face, orally mediated exchange; written exchanges mediated by print; and electronically

20. Bolter, *Writing Space* (above, n. 2), p. 3.

21. Ibid., p. 161.

22. Ibid., p. 162.

23. Ibid., p. 166.

24. Ibid.

mediated exchange. If the first stage is characterized by symbolic correspon-
dences, and the second stage is characterized by the representation of signs,
the third is characterized by informational simulations. In the first, oral stage
the self is constituted as a position of enunciation through its embeddedness
in a totality of face-to-face relations. In the second, print stage the self is
constructed as an agent centered in rational/imaginary autonomy. In the
third, electronic stage the self is decentered, dispersed, and multiplied in
continuous instability.[25]

Like his fellow electronic theorists, Poster proclaims that electronic
writing "disperses the [authorial] subject so that it no longer functions as a center in the way it did in pre-electronic writing."[26] But
like Bolter, he is divided on the question of deconstruction's ade-
quacy to electronic writing. Thus his discussion of Derrida and
electronic writing takes up the following question: "does the introduction of computer writing herald a stage of communication un-
foreseen and unaccountable by Derrida's method of textual deconstruction, or does deconstruction itself rather open theoretical
analysis to computer writing by destabilizing, subverting or complicating writing in a pre-electronic age?"[27] Although Poster is reluctant to come down completely on either side, the chapter is heavily
weighted toward the position that deconstruction does not satisfac-
torily account for the introduction of computer writing. In particular, the Derridean concept of the trace is seen as unable to account
for the immateriality of electronic writing. In computer writing,
Poster contends, "The writer . . . confronts a representation that is
similar in its spatial fragility and temporal simultaneity to the contents of the mind or the spoken word."[28] Because the "marks or
traces [of computer writing] are as evanescent as pixels on the
screen," and because such writing, "instantaneously available over
the globe, inserts itself in a nonlinear temporality that unsettles the
relation to the writing subject," Poster concludes that computer
writing "challenges and radicalizes the terms of analysis initiated
by the deconstructionist."[29]

   As persuasive as Poster's critique might appear, it overlooks the
fact that for Derrida the concept of the trace suggests that "the contents of the mind or the spoken word" are no less forms of writing

25. Poster, *Mode of Information* (above, n. 2), p. 6.

26. Ibid., p. 100.

27. Ibid., p. 99.

28. Ibid., p. 111.

29. Ibid., pp. 127–128.

for their "spatial fragility and temporal simultaneity." Like his fellow electronic theorists, Poster fails to recognize that the force of the Derridean critique is to demonstrate the way in which thought and speech are always already forms of writing. Deconstruction does not need to be instantiated or embodied in new electronic technologies; for Derrida, writing is always a technology and already electronic.[30] A similar misreading has developed in regard to Barthes's poststructuralist distinctions between "work" and "text," or between "readerly" and "writerly" texts, both of which distinctions are also habitually cited as theoretical anticipations of the technology of electronic writing. For Barthes, as for Derrida, however, the "writerly" "text" is always already immaterial, allusive, and intertextual—even in print. This is not to deny that in electronic writing the "work" has taken a different form, one that seems more closely to resemble the Barthesian "text." But in describing hypertext or electronic writing as embodying the assumptions of Barthesian poststructuralism or Derridean deconstruction, electronic enthusiasts run the risk of fetishizing the "work," of mistaking the "work" for the "text," the physical manifestation (electronic technologies) for the linguistic or discursive text—as when Bolter claims that "electronic text is the first text in which the elements of meaning, of structure, and of visual display are fundamentally unstable."[31] The force of the deconstructive and poststructuralist critiques is to illustrate the way in which this destabilization is true of all writing. To think otherwise is not to instantiate or embody these critiques but to mistake or ignore them.[32]

30. See Jacques Derrida, *Of Grammatology*, trans. Gayatri Spivak (Baltimore: Johns Hopkins University Press, 1976), for example, in the chapter entitled "The End of the Book and the Beginning of Writing," where Derrida notes: "And thus we say 'writing' for all that gives rise to an inscription in general, whether it is literal or not and even if what it distributes in space is alien to the order of the voice: cinematography, choreography, of course, but also pictorial, musical, sculptural 'writing'" (p. 9). For Derrida, the kind of nonphoneticized writing represented by the digitization of information in computer technology already exists in any number of different forms. He locates this kind of writing throughout the epoch of the logocentric metaphysics of presence; it is not a form of writing awaiting a new technology.

31. Bolter, *Writing Space* (above, n. 2), p. 31.

32. In Roland Barthes, *S/Z*, trans. Richard Miller (New York: Hill and Wang, 1974), pp. 4–5, Barthes contrasts "readerly" and "writerly" texts, noting that writerly texts can only be found "by accident, fleetingly, obliquely in certain limit-works . . . : the writerly text is not a thing, we would have a hard time finding it in a bookstore." Of course, he does not mean that the writerly text could be more easily found in a computer store, or on the Internet. Rather, as in his discussion of the *punctum* and *studium* in photography (in Roland Barthes, *Camera Lucida: Reflections on Photography*,

Poster reserves his harshest criticism of Derridean deconstruction, however, not for its failure to account for electronic writing, but for its failure to provide a politically useful contribution "to the work of critical social theory, to its reconstructive task of analyzing late twentieth-century society."[33] Because Derrida repeatedly refuses to provide "an examination in depth of the context of his own writing"—by which Poster means "the social context of computer writing"—he can only witness "from the outside the 'more profound reversal' of electronic writing."[34] Like Landow's and Bolter's, Poster's analysis of electronic writing relies heavily on its unproblematic characterization as immaterial, ephemeral, evanescent. The problem with this characterization, however, is that these ephemeral electromagnetic traces are dependent on extremely material hardware, software, communication networks, institutional and corporate structures, support personnel, and so on. In accounting for the social context of electronic writing, Poster (like other electronic theorists) repeatedly elides these very material, human, and technological contexts. This elision is emblematized in the following sentence from the book's introduction: "In principle," he writes, "information is now instantly available all over the globe and may be stored and retrieved as long as electricity is available."[35] In the movement of this sentence from "in principle" to "as long as electricity is available," Poster would elide virtually all of the important elements of the "social context of computer writing" that would seem to be the object of a truly "critical social theory." Ironically, this sentence serves also to remind us of the way in which, while fetishizing the physical manifestation of textual form, the discursive logic of electronic writing habitually elides or marginalizes the material, technological context of electronic writing, even when the issue at stake is whether or how these new technologies alter or change current social, institutional, or political practices. In the next section I take up two interrelated aspects of the claim for practical consequences of electronic writing: the claim that the new

trans. Richard Howard [New York: Hill and Wang, 1981]), the accidental quality of "writerly" texts does not operate (as readerly texts do) according to a purposive semiotic structure. As with Derrida, Barthes is describing conditions of writing already present in print technology. Just as we already have writerly texts in print, so we would not have to strain our imaginations to come up with multiple examples of electronic texts that have all of the characteristics of the readerly.

33. Poster, *Mode of Information* (above, n. 2), p. 110.

34. Ibid., pp. 108, 110.

35. Ibid., p. 2.

technologies demand a radical reconfiguration of humanities education; and the claim that the new technologies democratize writing and text-production (the question of politics).

Of the four authors under discussion, Landow and Lanham are the most enthusiastic proponents of the consequences of electronic writing for humanities education. For Landow, hypertext does for education what it has been seen to do for writing: "electronic hypertext," he writes, "challenges now conventional assumptions about teachers, learners, and the institutions they inhabit."[36] He sees hypertext as leading to a fundamental reconfiguration of the practices of traditional education—breaking down the distinction between teacher and student, redistributing time allocation, encouraging collaboration, making students more active, and providing expert material to novices. "Hypertext, by holding out the possibility of newly empowered, self-directed students, demands that we confront an entire range of questions about our conceptions of literary education."[37] But despite these enthusiastic proclamations, and despite the quite interesting ongoing educational applications of hypertext that Landow describes, he is not optimistic about the short-term possibilities for hypertextual education. Hypertext is unlikely to produce "dramatic changes in educational practice for some time to come," he argues, "in large part because of the combination of technological conservatism and general lack of concern with pedagogy that characterize the faculty at most institutions of higher learning, particularly at those that have pretensions to prestige."[38] While this may be an accurate characterization of his own peer group, it is not clear that it is equally true of the current generation of academic faculty, many of whose careers have been led by interest, inclination, and economic exigencies into concerns both with computer technologies and with pedagogy. Indeed, economic and class concerns would seem to suggest another major stumbling block to the implementation of hypertextual education: funding. Landow fails to consider the economic consequences of his proposals—not only the costs of obtaining, maintaining, and upgrading hardware and software for faculty and students, but also the costs of keeping class sizes at a reasonable level. Despite his reservations about faculty at institutions with "pretensions to prestige," his educational utopia takes as its model his own situation at Brown Uni-

36. Landow, *Hypertext* (above, n. 2), p. 120.

37. Ibid.

38. Ibid., pp. 160–161.

versity, where he describes his own classes of sixteen and twenty students, far fewer than those in similar classes at less prestigious institutions. Although Landow contends "that the history of information technology from writing to hypertext reveals an increasing democratization or dissemination of power," in his discussions of the pedagogical and political consequences of hypertext, class and economics are invisible.

The same is true of Richard Lanham's treatment of politics and pedagogy in *The Electronic Word,* a work that Bolter heralds as a first step toward a "positive theory" of electronic writing. For Lanham, as for Landow, the politics of the electronic word is radically democratic: "Digitization of the arts," Lanham writes, "radically democratizes them."[39] Further, "the people who developed the personal computer considered it a device of radical democratization from its inception."[40] Like Langdon Winner, Lanham believes that artifacts do have politics, that there are "assumptions that come with a book: it is authoritative and unchangeable, transparent and unselfconscious, read in silence and, if possible, in private. And we see the particular kind of literary and cultural decorum, and hence self and society, it implies much more clearly too."[41] For Lanham, these assumptions are particularly evident in the textbooks we find in our elementary and secondary schools: "These volumes—physically ugly, worn out if distributed in the public schools, bound in vile peanut-butter-sandwich-proof pyroxeline covers, unmarked since unowned, written in a prose style intentionally dumbed down by readability formulae which filter out all the pleasures of prose, written of course to offend no one—these volumes do a terrific job of teaching students to hate reading."[42] Contrast this state of things, he writes, with "interactive video-and-text-programs, based on laser-optical techniques": "An interactive compact laser disk can hold one thousand video stills, two thousand diagrams, six hours of high-quality sound, ten thousand pages of text, and have enough space left over to make it all work together."[43] Such technologies lead Lanham (as others) to dream:

> Imagine a major "textbook," continuing over a generation, [he urges,] continually in touch with all the teachers who use it, continually updated and rewritten by them as well as by the "authors," with the twenty-four-hour

39. Lanham, *Electronic Word* (above, n. 2), p. 107

40. Ibid., p. 108.

41. Ibid., p. 8.

42. Ibid., p. 9.

43. Ibid., pp. 9–10.

electronic bulletin boards and the other one-to-one devices of communication such a network inevitably stimulates. Imagine a department faculty collaborating to produce a full on-line system of primary and secondary texts, with supporting pedagogical apparatus, to be collectively updated and enhanced; it might encourage a real, and nowadays rare, collegiality.[44]

It is hard to deny the appeal of Lanham's Lennon-like "imagination" of the electronic textbook. But as powerful, attractive, and desirable as this image is, and as depressing and unacceptable as his picture of current textbook-based education may be, the claim that "electronic 'textbooks' are democratizing education in all the arts,"[45] like the claim that "the electronic word democratizes the world of arts and letters,"[46] transfers political agency from people to things, from cultural practices to machines. In so doing, Lanham can easily overlook the fact that the current state of elementary, secondary, and postsecondary education is a consequence not only, not even primarily, of the technologies of writing they employ, but of the priorities we as a nation place upon education. It seems equally certain that as new electronic technologies continue to be installed in our schools, they will be installed not "democratically," but by means of the same kind of trickle-down economics under which American education operated throughout the 1980s.

Or will they? Lanham's and Landow's discussions (and the questions I have raised about them) have all operated according to what Bruno Latour has described as the "diffusion model" of explaining the dissemination of technoscience. In this model, new technologies like electronic writing or hypertext are seen to succeed or fail based on their own agency, not on the agency of the people and institutions who have taken them up. Latour describes two bizarre consequences of this fairly common explanation of the dissemination of new technologies: "First, it seems that as people so easily agree to transmit the object, it is the object itself that forces them to assent. It then seems that the behavior of people is *caused* by the diffusion of facts and machines. It is forgotten that the obedient behavior of people is what turns the claims into facts and machines; the careful strategies that give the object the contours that will provide assent are also forgotten."[47] For Latour, the diffusion

44. Ibid., p. 10.

45. Ibid.

46. Ibid., p. 23.

47. Bruno Latour, *Science in Action: How to Follow Scientists and Engineers through Society* (Cambridge, Mass.: Harvard University Press, 1987), p. 133.

model "invents a technical determinism, paralleled by a scientific determinism."[48] The conjunction of these two determinisms produces a

> second consequence . . . as bizarre as the first. Since facts [like machines] are now endowed with an inertia that does not depend on the action of people or on that of their many non-human allies, what propels them? To solve this question adepts of the diffusion model have to invent a new mating system. Facts [like machines] are supposed to reproduce one another! Forgotten are the many people who carry them from hand to hand, the crowds of acting entities that shape the facts and are shaped by them, the complex negotiations to decide which association is stronger or weaker.[49]

The diffusion model operates according to what David Bloor has christened the "principle of asymmetry," in which society and culture are seen to enter the picture only when something goes wrong, to explain why it did not work: "society is simply a medium of different resistances *through which* ideas and machines travel."[50] The failure of electronic writing technologies to have universally and immediately transformed humanities education, for example, would be accounted for in the diffusion model "in terms of the resistance, the passivity or ignorance of the local [academic] culture. Society or 'social factors' would appear only at the end of the trajectory, when something went wrong. This has been called the principle of *asymmetry*: there is appeal to social factors only when the true path of reason has been 'distorted' but not when it goes straight."[51] This principle is evident in both Landow and Lanham, who seem to ascribe agency to academic faculty and administrators almost exclusively in their guise as Luddites. "Humanists are such natural Luddites," Lanham writes, "and have become so used to regarding technology—and especially the computer—as the enemy that it takes some temerity to call the personal computer a friend."[52] In the relations among theory, technology, and society described by Landow and Lanham, factors like class and economics, or agents like individuals or society, are seen, not as the cause of the proliferation of electronic writing technologies within elementary, secondary, and postsecondary humanities education, but

48. Ibid.
49. Ibid.
50. Ibid., p. 136.
51. Ibid.
52. Lanham, *Electronic Word* (above, n. 2), p. 23.

only as possible obstacles to the more complete dissemination of these new technologies.

If what I am claiming is indeed the case, that the discursive logic of electronic authorship simultaneously ascribes agency to and elides technology, then how are we to make sense of this failure to account for the materiality of electronic technologies, their imbrication in a multitude of economic, social, and cultural contexts? How can scholars who celebrate the democratizing possibilities of the new technologies fail to take into consideration their materiality, their economic and social costs?

One way to begin to make sense of this failure is to look at the recurrent trope of dematerialization used to represent the consequence of electronic technologies. For Lanham, as for Poster, digitization produces desubstantiation: "Digitization is desubstantiating the whole world of the visual arts. This common digital denominator of the arts and letters forces upon us a rhetoric of the arts like none seen before."[53] Because all arts can be digitized, Lanham contends, they can be simultaneously desubstantiated and transformed both into a common language and into each other: "Digitization gives [the arts] a new common ground, a quasi-mathematical equivalency that recalls the great Platonic dream for the unity of all knowledge. Digitization both desubstantiates a work of art and subjects it to perpetual immanent metamorphosis from one sense-dimension to another."[54] Like Poster's vision of electronic writing's dematerialization of the subject, Lanham's desubstantiated utopia would elide both the programmer and the program-code, along with all of the culturally constructed assumptions by which sound and sight can be translated into digits and into each other—assumptions that are anything but simply mathematical or "quasi-mathematical." Lanham's elision of the material and social context of the computer (including, but not limited to, programmer, hardware, and software) is clear in a sentence inserted in the midst of a discussion of computerized programs for turning geometric drawings into music. Celebrating the way in which such programs make musical composition "available to performers without formal music training," Lanham parenthetically qualifies: "(The computer training required is something else.)"[55] This parenthetical "something else" stands for what Lanham and others fail repeatedly to

53. Ibid., pp. 3–4.

54. Ibid., p. 11.

55. Ibid., p. 12.

theorize: the material, economic, cultural basis of this digital de-substantiation.

This elision of the material and cultural basis of electronic writing seems inconsistent with that aspect of the logic of electronic authorship that foregrounds the causal role of technologies. In noting that entities like writing, literature, authorship, or texts are seen not as neutral, transcendent, or disembodied, but as constituted by the particular technologies in which they are materialized, electronic theorists would call attention to the constitutive or determining role of technologies of writing or information. The logic of electronic authorship that I have been mapping out depends in the first instance upon the rhetorical move of historicizing technologies. To then imagine that current technologies of (and like) writing are destabilized by pointing out that they have histories is only to suggest that since things used to be different, they could be again. That is, to point out that literary or cultural or humanistic knowledge is technologically constructed is seen to lay the basis for a potentially significant challenge to the Western tradition's assumption of disinterested knowledge.

Unfortunately, theories of electronic writing seem only to reproduce the fundamental logical oppositions that structure this tradition. The discursive logic of electronic authorship seems almost invariably to marginalize or elide its own central insights, either by making the technology itself transparent or by eliding the complicated discursive relationships between knowledge and power. While the logic of electronic writing that I have been tracing out depends upon the insight that the forms and content of liberal humanism are technologically constructed, it seems blind to the analogous insight that the great truths of the Western tradition are culturally constructed as well. William Paulson has attempted to explain this phenomenon, arguing that digitization and desubstantiation of the texts of Western culture strips them from their cultural and social context.[56] Because all information can be translated into digital code, can be made to appear on the screen in the same format as all other information, Paulson contends that electronic technologies are inevitably decontextualizing technologies. In so arguing, however, he reproduces the technological fallacy by ascribing agency to the technology itself. To imagine that digitally reproducing texts from two different historical contexts would decontextualize them is both to fetishize technology by making an idol of

56. William Paulson, "Computers, Minds, and Texts: Preliminary Reflections," *New Literary History* 20 (Winter 1989): 291–303.

the "form" in which writing is commodified, and to fetishize the particular historical context in which those texts were reproduced. Electronic information technologies do not *de*contextualize the texts of Western culture, they *re*contextualize them. Thus, rather than celebrating or lamenting electronic writing for decontextualizing or desubstantializing the great texts of Western print culture, we need to analyze the cultural work that electronic writing can do and already does.

In arguing for the cultural work performed by electronic writing, I do not mean to be taken as inverting the technological fallacy into a cultural fallacy, as suggesting that instead of considering technology as an agent of cultural change, we should consider culture as an agent of technological change. Rather, I would contend that the characterization of electronic writing as unstable, ephemeral, or dematerialized needs to be carefully reconsidered. Following the lead of Latour's analysis of technoscience in action, I would suggest that to understand what is new and different about electronic authorship, we need to look at the way in which the network of inscriptions that constitute electronic writing circulates within a heterogeneous social space of cultural, linguistic, and technoscientific practices. In calling for thick historical or ethnographic descriptions of the circulation of electronic writing within this heterogeneous social space, I want to insist with Latour that technoscience and culture are not distinct, autonomous realms capable of "acting" upon one another but interrelated realms in which action is always made possible through the association of heterogeneous elements, in which technology and culture are organized through heterogeneous networks of strength, power, and alliance rather than separated into homogeneous, even if intersecting or interrelated, realms. Once we begin to pay careful attention to the circulation of electronic writing within these heterogeneous networks, I am confident that we will begin to realize that what finally makes electronic writing so remarkable is not its immateriality but rather its power to marshal such a diversity of material, cultural, and technological forces. Like print, but more powerfully and materially, the technologies of electronic writing function at what Latour calls "centers of calculation" to appropriate, incorporate, and control the heterogeneous network of cultural, linguistic, and technoscientific practices that constitute information capitalism at the end of the twentieth century.[57]

---

57. Latour, *Science in Action* (above, n. 47), chap. 6.

Boundaries: Mathematics, Alienation, and the Metaphysics of Cyberspace

Robert Markley

I

To listen to its proponents, one would think that cyberspace has no past. Since William Gibson coined the term in *Neuromancer*, his "consensual hallucination" has become almost a brand name for life in the postmodern, postindustrial age—a cyborg existence irrevocably dependent on technological interventions in and augmentations of our bodies.[1] Most descriptions of cyberspace emphasize that it is, in Michael Benedikt's words, "a new stage, a new and irresistible development in the elaboration of human culture and business under the sign of technology."[2] For Benedikt and for many others, the role of breakthrough technologies in restructuring human nature is axiomatic.[3] Those involved in developing virtual technologies—our ports of entry to cyberspace—are usually upbeat about this reconstruction of the self and society. Throughout the growing literature on cyberspace, as discussed in my introduction to this collection, cybernauts present the integrative technologies of Virtual Reality as an almost phenomenological means to heal the ruptures within our postmodern, postindustrial identities.[4]

1. William Gibson, *Neuromancer* (New York: Berkley, 1984), p. 7.

2. Michael Benedikt, "Introduction," in *Cyberspace: First Steps,* ed. idem (Cambridge, Mass.: MIT Press, 1991), p. 1.

3. See, for example, Meredith Bricken, "Virtual Worlds: No Interface to Design," in Benedikt, *Cyberspace,* pp. 363–382.

4. See Margaret A. Rose, *The Post-Modern and the Post-Industrial: A Critical Analysis* (Cambridge: Cambridge University Press, 1991).

Paradoxically, they contend, accepting our fate as cyborgs will allow us to become more fully human, to free our inherently creative natures from the belatedness, the alienation, of representation.[5] If many cyberpunk writers (and critics) regard our electronically mediated future with suspicion, those involved in developing virtual systems characteristically promote cyberspace as a technological panacea for our postmodern malaise.

I want to begin my critique of this view by suggesting a more guarded approach to virtual technologies—and a different definition of cyberspace. Cyberspace is a consensual cliché, a dumping ground for repackaged philosophies about space, subjectivity, and culture; it does not offer a breakthrough in human, or cyborgian, evolution, but merely (though admittedly) a seductive means to reinscribe fundamental tensions within Western concepts of identity and reality. I remain skeptical of the notion that a technologically mediated existence offers a radical break with our "modernist" past, and suspicious of the leaps of faith we are asked to make from experimental, jury-rigged, and often gremlin-ridden virtual technologies to the nearly mystical unity of human and machine in cyberspace. In my mind, there is nothing necessarily "irresistible" about the development of cyberspace; rather than a consensual hallucination, it represents a contested and irrevocably political terrain that is unlikely to determine the future "elaboration of human culture." My critique of cyberspace, then, is concerned less with the problems of access to new technologies (though an analysis of the ideology of informatics, as Donna Haraway, Anne Balsamo, and Gary Chapman have demonstrated, is crucial to a democratic politics in the age of information) than with the largely unchallenged discourses of the metaphysics of cyberspace—the philosophizing that ignores or mystifies the theoretical and historical underpinnings of this hallucinatory realm and that consequently downplays the technological and political difficulties involved in creating and disseminating virtual worlds.[6] My purpose, I would emphasize, is

5. See, for example, Nicole Stenger, "Mind is a Leaking Rainbow," in Benedikt, *Cyberspace* (above, n. 2), pp. 49–58; and Timothy Leary, "The Cyberpunk: The Individual as Reality Pilot," in *Storming the Reality Studio: A Casebook of Cyberpunk and Postmodern Science Fiction*, ed. Larry McCaffery (Durham, N.C.: Duke University Press, 1991), pp. 249–258. On the problems of representation in science, see Steve Woolgar, *Science: The Very Idea* (London: Tavistock, 1988).

6. On problems of access to virtual technologies, see Donna Haraway, *Simians, Cyborgs, and Women: The Reinvention of Nature* (New York: Routledge, 1991); Anne Balsamo, "Feminism for the Incurably Informed," *South Atlantic Quarterly* 92 (1993): 681–712; and Gary Chapman, "Taming the Computer," *South Atlantic Quarterly* 92

not to attack the development of virtual technologies, but to suggest that their usefulness in education, medicine, architecture, art, engineering, and other fields depends precisely on our resistance to their being collapsed into "cyberspace"—the naive, totalizing incarnation of Western tendencies to privilege mind over materiality.[7]

Many of the people involved in developing the software and hardware for virtual technologies are deeply, often vocally, suspicious of the motives and expertise of cultural critics intent on colonizing cyberspace. Like other scientists, many have retreated to the bulwarks of technological literacy to defend their positive, even utopian, views of what virtual technologies will mean for humankind.[8] Significantly, however, the scientific and technical literature on cyberspace is framed consistently, often unapologetically, in a millenarian rhetoric that, recasting the legacy of the 1960s counterculture, celebrates a technology that promises rewards exceeding the expenditures of labor and capital required to bring it into being. Cyberspace, in effect, *is* a metaphysical construct, shot through with the assumptions and values of an idealist philosophy. Its proponents, from Michael Benedikt to Timothy Leary, favor rhetorical jump cuts between technological jargon and mystical incantations: these leaps of faith from the still-primitive technologies of virtual reality to the fictional realm of a seamless human-machine symbiosis are conditioned by the binary structures of thought that characterize traditional views of science and metaphysics. Typically, the literature of cyberspace (as distinct from the cultural criticism of cyberpunk) proceeds as though deconstructive,

(1993): 827–850. For skeptical treatments of the values that cyberspace reinscribes, see Allucquère Rosanne Stone, "Will the Real Body Please Stand Up? Boundary Stories about Virtual Cultures," in Benedikt, *Cyberspace* (above, n. 2), pp. 81–118; and Kathleen Biddick, "Humanist History and the Haunting of Virtual Worlds: Problems of Memory and Rememoration," *Genders* 18 (1993): 47–66.

7. For some of the uses of virtual technologies, see Marcus Novak, "Liquid Architecture in Cyberspace," in Benedikt, *Cyberspace*, pp. 225–254; Chris Byrne, *Virtual Reality and Education,* Technical Publication No. R-93-6 (Seattle: Human Interface Technology Laboratory of the Washington Technology Center, 1993); and Kimberley Oberg, *Virtual Reality and Education: A Look at Both Sides of the Sword,* Technical Publication No. R-93-7 (Seattle: Human Interface Technology Laboratory, 1993). See also Toni Emerson, *Selected Bibliography on Virtual Interface Technology,* Technical Publication No. B-93-2 (Seattle: Human Interface Technology Laboratory of the Washington Technology Center, 1993).

8. On the practitioners and proponents of Virtual Reality, see Howard Rheingold, *Virtual Reality* (New York: Simon and Schuster), 1991; on the response of some scientists to cultural criticism, see Paul Gross and Norman Levitt, *Higher Superstition: The Academic Left and Its Quarrels with Science* (Baltimore: Johns Hopkins University Press, 1994).

feminist, and radical critiques of that tradition did not exist.[9]

In brief, cyberspace seems so familiar, so "natural" and "irresistible" a development, because it reproduces what Jean-Joseph Goux describes as the sexualized oppositions—mind/body, form/content, idea/matter, male/female, and so on—that have characterized Western thought since (at least) Plato.[10] Although the developers and popularizers of virtual technologies employ a variety of arguments to justify their enthusiasm, they share a romantic emphasis on the creative potential of the subject; a Platonic idealism fundamental to the philosophy of mathematics; progressivist, often overtly teleological, assumptions about the historical development of science and technology; and a liberal humanist view of the individual as inherently free to choose his or her options in a reconfigured space that symbolizes democratic and capitalist principles. My analysis, then, begins with an overwhelming irony: in cyberspace, we confront a radically constructivist technology that celebrates an undisguised essentialism.

Cyberspace provokes often-rapturous rhetoric but resists critical analysis, I would suggest, because most of its commentators have either accepted uncritically, or failed to grapple with, its conceptual foundations in late twentieth-century mathematics. As Benjamin Woolley argues, at the heart of cyberspace lies a fundamental belief in the mathematical structure of nature, in the computability of the universe.[11] The idea that the world can be understood through mathematics—that mathematics is the alphabet of creation—goes back at least to the seventeenth century; ultimately, it is a belief in the aesthetics of a natural order that can be revealed in and by mathematics and then reproduced—and heightened—in virtual worlds.[12] In much of the technical literature on virtual systems, I

9. On cyberpunk, see John Christie, "A Tragedy for Cyborgs," *Configurations* 1 (1993): 171–196; David Porush, "Frothing the Synaptic Bath: What Puts the Punk in Cyberpunk?" in *Fiction 2000,* ed. George Slusser and Thomas Shippey (Athens: University of Georgia Press, 1992) pp. 246–261; Istvan Csicsery-Ronay, "Futuristic Flu, or, The Revenge of the Future," in ibid., pp. 26–45; Pam Rosenthal, "Jacked In: Fordism, Cyberpunk, Marxism," *Socialist Review* 21 (1991): 79–105; and Thomas Foster, "Incurably Informed: The Pleasures and Dangers of Cyberpunk," *Genders* 18 (1993): 1–10. On the critique of metaphysics, see particularly Jean-Joseph Goux, *Symbolic Economies after Marx and Freud,* trans. Jennifer Curtiss Gage (Ithaca, N.Y.: Cornell University Press, 1990).

10. Goux, *Symbolic Economies,* esp. pp. 223–236.

11. Benjamin Woolley, *Virtual Worlds: A Journey in Hype and Hyperreality* (New York: Penguin, 1992), esp. pp. 247–254.

12. See Robert Markley, *Fallen Languages: Crises of Representation in Newtonian England, 1660–1740* (Ithaca, N.Y.: Cornell University Press, 1993), pp. 131–144, 185–197.

suggest, mathematics both describes the formal structure of cyber-space and functions (to borrow Nancy Leys Stepan's term) as the "constitutive metaphor" of virtual worlds.[13] Because, in this view, mathematics reveals an underlying symmetry—a harmony—to the universe, it is not a form of representation but of revelation: the mythic structure of cyberspace is based on the identification of mathematics and metaphysical order that has persisted from Pythagoras to quantum physics.[14] If mathematics, then, is both an instrument and an expression of faith, it informs what Michael Heim suggests is the "erotic ontology" of cyberspace, an erotics at once individualistic and communitarian; this erotics, in the words of Jaron Lanier, "gives us a sense of being able to be who we are without limitation, for our imagination to become objective and shared with other people."[15] In this respect, the claims made for cy-berspace—that it reveals an "essential" harmony within the ecolo-gy of the self; that it transcends the mind-body split; that it moves beyond representation to an erotics of self-presence; and that it provides for a shared and objective imagination—seek to body forth a latter-day Leibnizian monadology which, to be at all con-vincing, must attempt to decontextualize the technologies that bring cyberspace into being. This process of decontextualization both shapes and is shaped by the mathematical underpinnings of virtual worlds. A working definition: cyberspace is the idealized projection of the values and assumptions, the seemingly founda-tional principles, of the mathematics of advanced number-crunch-ing on which virtual technologies depend. I would argue, then, that we need to examine the theoretical foundations of the compu-tational structures of Virtual Reality, because it is at this naturalized level of the mathematically "true" that these principles are encod-ed.

II

One of the leading figures in the development of Virtual Reality software is William Bricken, formerly of the Human Interface Tech-nology Laboratory at the University of Washington, and before that

13. Nancy Leys Stepan, "Race and Gender: The Role of Analogy in Science," *Isis* 77 (1986): 261–277. See also James Bono, "Science, Discourse, and Literature: The Role/Rule of Metaphor in Science," in *Literature and Science: Theory and Practice,* ed. Stuart Peterfreund (Boston: Northeastern University Press, 1990), pp. 59–90.

14. On mathematics and order, see Morris Kline, *Mathematics: The Loss of Certainty* (New York: Oxford University Press, 1980).

15. Michael Heim, "The Erotic Ontology of Cyberspace," in Benedikt, *Cyberspace* (above, n. 2), pp. 59–80; Jaron Lanier, quoted in Woolley, *Virtual Worlds* (above, n. 11), p. 14.

one of the researchers—along with Brenda Laurel, Jaron Lanier, Scott Fisher, and Warren Robinett—who began working on virtual systems at Atari's Sunnyvale research facility in the early 1980s.[16] In addition to writing a number of technical reports published by the HIT Lab, Bricken is responsible for some of the more Zen-like pronouncements coming from the community of researchers working on virtual technologies: "psychology is the physics of virtual reality," he has stated, and "reality is in the eye of the beholder."[17] However "unscientific" these statements may seem, they are less expressions of a puzzling new faith, as Woolley implies, than of a resourceful extension of a mathematically based philosophy: boundary logic. The crucial problem that Bricken and others face in designing virtual systems is how to process vast amounts of information as quickly as possible; on a technical level, Virtual Reality depends on almost instantaneous feedback of billions of bits of information that can be translated into direct sensory input to allow virtual environments to move around us as we move through them. Bricken's ongoing solution to the daunting computational problems posed by virtual systems has been to develop a "simplified propositional logic," derived from G. Spencer-Brown's *Laws of Form*, the crucial (and only) text in the controversial field of boundary mathematics.[18]

Boundary mathematics allows for the rapid, deductive transformation of complicated mathematical expressions into radically simplified forms. What Spencer-Brown terms his Calculus of Indications depends on our recognition of the originary significance of a new mathematical symbol, the "mark." The mark, as Meredith Bricken describes it, "is the *only object* and the *only operator*" in this calculus; it indicates "a cluster of attributes: it is a distinction and the observer making the distinction; it is a boundary and an instruction to cross that boundary; it is a symbol and a process, a name and a value. The mark exists in a context of continuous space; it generates systems and determines their functioning."[19] As

16. Woolley, *Virtual Worlds*, p. 17.

17. Quoted in ibid., p. 21.

18. G. Spencer-Brown, *The Laws of Form* (London: Macmillan, 1969). On the controversy over boundary mathematics, see Paul Cull and William Frank, "Flaws of Form," *International Journal of General Systems* 5 (1979): 201–211; Francisco Varela, "A Calculus for Self-Reference," *International Journal of General Systems* 2 (1975): 5–24; and B. Banaschewski, "On G. Spencer-Brown's *Laws of Form*," *Notre Dame Journal of Formal Logic* 18 (1977): 507–509.

19. Meredith Bricken, *A Calculus of Creation*, Technical Publication No. HITL-P-91-3 (Seattle: Human Interface Technology Laboratory of the Washington Technology Center, [1991]), p. [1].

her rhetoric suggests, the mark is both a notational device and a metaphysical marker of one's unique location in the "continuous context" of space.[20]

In discussing the significance of the *Laws of Form*, Meredith Bricken describes the underlying philosophical assumptions of this latter-day, Leibnizian monadology: the investment of mathematical notation with metaphysical significance. She suggests that "the exploration of the mark begins" with self-reflection, "the simple awareness of being" that allows one to perceive oneself as both a boundary and a process of transition between "inside" and "outside."[21] But in a monadological universe, the continuous space that she describes, one's "awareness of [oneself] as a distinction is all that exists"; therefore, to make a mark (such as a circle formed by one's thumb and forefinger) is to reproduce the primary distinction between inside and outside: "Behold (be, see, hold) this form as a distinction in space. Your gesture is another mark. It is a functional duplicate of the primal mark you yourself form in space, an object/process distinguishing 'inside' from 'outside.' "[22] This self-referential nature of the mark is crucial because it allows Spencer-Brown and the Brickens to identify this arbitrary notational distinction with the intention—even the existence—of the observer: "the first distinction, the mark, and the observer," Spencer-Brown maintains, "are not only interchangeable but in the form identical."[23] The mark, then, is always the projection of an observer's perspective, and consequently, because the observer both creates and is the mark, he or she can "assign it any value."[24] Value is always an expression of intention. Form, identity, and value thus are generated by the intentional, Ur-statements of boundary logic: I mark, therefore I am; I am the mark, therefore I am.

In the context of an empty space, distinctions (and intentions) are theoretically infinite; as Spencer-Brown declares, "any form of reference [can] be divisible without limits."[25] But significantly, in boundary mathematics, these distinctions do not proliferate into multiple perspectives. Axiom 1 of the Calculus of Indications— "calling"—is a principle of identity: to call is to make a mark, and calling is a self-identical rather than cumulative process: "one dis-

20. Ibid., p. [3].

21. Ibid., p. [1].

22. Ibid., p. [2].

23. Spencer-Brown, *Laws of Form* (above, n. 18), p. 76.

24. M. Bricken, *Calculus* (above, n. 19), p. [5].

25. Spencer-Brown, *Laws of Form*, p. 10.

tinction [or mark] is the same as two distinctions; it is equivalent to three or four or any number of distinctions."[26] Functionally, a space can be marked, but it cannot be marked again. If we take a circle as the primal mark, then calling can be represented as follows:

$$O \; O \; O = O$$

Axiom 2—"crossing"—holds that "recrossing a boundary is the same as never having crossed it."[27] One can be "inside" the mark or "outside" of it; one can call and cross indefinitely, but one will always end up in one of two states: inside or outside.

William Bricken offers a "physical model" of these axioms:

> consider a door to a room. The intent of a door is to permit us to get to the other side. A duplicate door does not change the accessibility of the other side (CALLING). To go through a door and then to go through it again is the same as not having used it all (CROSSING). The intent of a lock is to cancel the intent of the door. To lock the door and then to lock it again does not change the locked state of the door (CALLING). To lock the door and then to unlock it is the same as not having locked it in the first place.[28]

Regardless of how many times one goes through the door, one ends up on either one side or the other. Ending up in your dining room one time or one thousand times is, in boundary logic, functionally identical. As Meredith Bricken puts it, "several marks are redundant in function; one mark serves the purpose."[29] This principle of redundancy is important because it allows for radical simplification in computational logic. Because any number of marks can be reduced to one of two states—calling: to maintain perspective, or crossing: to change perspective—boundary mathematics works "to eliminate descriptively irrelevant structure."[30] In parens notation, the axioms of boundary arithmetic can be expressed like this:

$$( ) \; ( ) = ( ) \quad \text{Calling}$$

$$(\; ( ) \;) = \qquad \text{Crossing}$$

---

26. M. Bricken, *Calculus,* p. [7].

27. Ibid., p. [8].

28. William Bricken, *An Introduction to Boundary Logic with the Losp Deductive Engine,* Technical Report No. HITL-R-89-1 (Seattle: Human Interface Technology Laboratory of the Washington Technology Center, [1989]), p. 8.

29. M. Bricken, *Calculus* (above, n. 19), p. [7].

30. W. Bricken, *Introduction* (above, n. 28), p. 7.

All logical and computational problems can be resolved through, and to, these axioms. More complicated expressions can always, in boundary logic, be simplified:

$$(\,(\,)\,) \quad \longrightarrow$$

$$(\,(\,(\,)\,)\,) \longrightarrow (\,)$$

These processes of simplification are deductive. They are not solutions to problems in an algebraic universe but operations of a propositional logic.

Following Spencer-Brown, William Bricken asserts that "CROSSING and CALLING form a *basis* for logic, providing sufficient structure to represent all constants and connectives, and to reduce all expressions without variables to a truth value."[31] From these axioms, he derives "transformation rules"—absorb, clarify, extract, and coalesce—that ensure "computational efficiency" through "deduction by reductive rewriting"; they "erase and *create* structure rather than rearrange tokens."[32] "Truth value," however, in boundary logic requires some explanation because it is both the grounds and the result of deductive transformation rules—a basic principle of structure. For Bricken, "true is associated with symbolic existence, ( ). This association is natural," he claims, "since the distinction is an indicator of our existence as symbol creators."[33] Therefore, "true" can be expressed by a "visually balanced equation":

$$(\,) = (\,)$$

In parens notation, this is the expression of identity. In contrast, "false" becomes "an association between absence of truth and absence of symbolism," expressed algebraically by a "visually unbalanced equation":[34]

$$= (\,)$$

"False," therefore, is a "non-represented concept . . . everywhere within a configuration, since the space with which it is identified underlies all symbols."[35] The "truth value" that Bricken discusses is

31. Ibid., p. 13.

32. Ibid., p. 9.

33. Ibid., p. 11.

34. Ibid.

35. Ibid., p. 9.

a function of a symbolic totality, of unmediated creation; "false" must be consigned to a "non-represented concept" precisely because it is the space of representation, of a material semiotics, against which symbols must define their truth-value as idealizations.

Crucially, boundary logic explicitly rejects linear forms of representation, which, according to William Bricken, impose "constraints upon mathematical thinking."[36] Rather than "distributive rules" and "sequential grouping and ordering rules," boundary mathematics allows "objects to *share* a space devoid of linear structure" and to "accommodate an *arbitrary number of arguments*, including none."[37] This "simple space" allows a single operator—add, subtract, divide, or multiply—to operate on all tokens within it simultaneously. To describe this space, the observer must exist formally within it so that any form of duplication—any (re)crossing of boundaries in this conceptual space—can be eliminated as redundant from his or her perspective. Because space can be perceived only from this perspective, linear relationships—cause and effect, for example—cannot obtain: "Since the space of representation [in boundary mathematics] is free of relationships, configurations within the same space do not interact and are freely decomposable."[38] Instead, boundary mathematics makes space itself functional, thereby incorporating the mathematician as "the fundamental mathematical construct."[39] In Bricken's simple space, then, truth-value and identity are functions of symbol-making, a process that is always intentional. "Self-observation," Bricken declares, "is at the core of simple symbols," and consequently he is able to treat "the equivalence between self-observation and non-representation as an axiom."[40] That is, the participant must be present to him or herself: he or she exists as both a function and an identity, as a symbolic whole.

Bricken's description of the axiomatic relationship between "self-observation and non-representation" forms the basis of his efforts to make boundary logic the mathematical structure and metaphysical validation of cyberspace. Because boundary mathematics is cen-

36. William Bricken, *A Simple Space,* Technical Report No. HITL-R-86-3 (Seattle: Human Interface Technology Laboratory of the Washington Technology Center, 1986), p. 1.

37. W. Bricken, *Introduction* (above, n. 28), p. 1.

38. Ibid., p. 13.

39. W. Bricken, *Simple Space* (above, n. 36), p. 14.

40. Ibid., pp. 15, 17.

tered on the participant/observer as its "fundamental construct," it "provides three critical tools for cyberspace: object/environment dualism, dynamic interaction, and pervasion."[41] The purpose of the Losp deductive engine, Bricken explains, is "to convert the foundations of mathematics (logic, set theory, integer theory) to experiential form"; given the underlying structure of the mathematics that he describes, his account of the virtues of cyberspace emphasizes that the participant in cyberspace exists in *"dynamic interaction with information"* and consequently "space (and experience) are *pervasive* rather than dualistic"—"both/and inclusions rather than either/or dichotomies."[42] In effect, cyberspace becomes an attempt both to embody the Laws of Form and to project the body as an ideal, materially unfettered, form in a simple space. As Heim suggests, in cyberspace, "the dream of perfect FORMS becomes the dream of inFORMation."[43] In its commitment to transcending dualistic structures, cyberspace recalls the seventeenth century's dreams of an Adamic language that is the signature—not the sign—of a mystical unity between the inscription and the perfect intelligence behind the inscription. And yet, ironically, the means that Bricken and others choose in order to move beyond representation, the mathematics of form, is rooted in the very binary thinking that it seeks to overcome.

I have explicated boundary mathematics at some length to suggest that the metaphysical presuppositions of cyberspace develop from and mimic the operations of a "simple propositional logic" that is designed to reduce complex expressions to simple statements. The transformation rules that Bricken describes, in effect, automate the computational and logical steps necessary to the parallel processing of information in virtual technologies. The Losp deductive engine thus provides a means to avoid having to recalculate and recalibrate inductively each shift in perspective, each new view, in Virtual Reality. But in addition to its usefulness in theorizing ways to simplify complex computational problems, "boundary philosophy" is also, as Bricken insists, "constructivist, innovative, and fundamental."[44] For its practitioners, boundary mathematics is not simply an instrumental practice but a "fundamental discovery"

41. William Bricken, *Extended Abstract: A Formal Foundation for Cyberspace*, Technical Report No. HITL-M-90-10 (Seattle: Human Interface Technology Laboratory of the Washington Technology Center, 1990), p. 2.

42. Ibid., pp. 2, 3.

43. Heim, "Erotic Ontology" (above, n. 15), p. 65.

44. W. Bricken, *Introduction* (above, n. 28), pp. 62–63.

that "meet[s] the mathematical criteria of clarity, completeness, and consistency . . . [and] the computational criteria of elegance, effectiveness, and efficiency."[45]

As the basis of cyberspace, then, boundary logic offers new "laws," new scientific truths, a new paradigm for analyzing and creating fundamental mathematical structures. The investment of the Brickens and others in the truth-value of boundary philosophy helps to explain why many proponents of virtual technologies have little patience with cultural critics who approach cyberspace through Gibson's novels and who emphasize the negative, even dystopian, effects of electronically mediated experience: for its proponents, cyberspace is not a fiction but an instantiation of true forms, real "laws." Consequently, articles by literary critics, no matter how astute, about cyberpunk, cyborg technologies, and the gendered nature of cyberspace are likely to have little effect on the people developing the software and hardware for virtual technologies because these critiques do not engage the "fundamental" beliefs (the mathematicizing of reality, self-observation) that inform cyberspace. What are at stake in fostering a more productive, if no less heated, debate between the practitioners and critics of cyberspace are political questions about power, knowledge, and experience raised by the development of virtual technologies. In what follows, then, I want to emphasize the ways in which boundary philosophy and cyberspace remain implicated in the re-production of a logic of alienation that divides the subject against herself and that renders her an effect of what I take to be the constitutive metaphors of virtual technologies: mathematics, the ideology of alienation, and capital.

III

Whatever advantages boundary logic may offer to the Brickens and their colleagues, their view of what mathematics is and what it describes remains traditional, even Platonic. As Brian Rotman argues, most practicing mathematicians are Platonists; they believe that numbers represent instrumentally simplified or model situations and that they are capable of revealing an underlying order and harmony to the universe. Distinguishing Platonism from formalism and intuitionism, Rotman argues that, for Platonists (who make up the vast majority of practicing mathematicians), mathematics is neither a

45. Ibid., p. 62.

game [formalism] nor some kind of languageless mental construction [intuitionism], but a science, a public discipline concerned to discover and validate objective or logical truths. According to this conception mathematical assertions are true or false propositions, statements of *facts* about some definite state of affairs, some objective reality, which exists independently of and prior to the mathematical act of investigating it.[46]

In a broadly Platonist framework, mathematics can—in fact, must—represent accurately real-world transactions and the truth-values that underlie them. The "objective reality" that mathematics describes, therefore, is predicated on the assumption that the universe itself is computable and that mathematics reveals its underlying harmony. As William Bricken's defense of boundary philosophy suggests, a mathematically described reality is constituted as "true" or "real" by the reflexive criteria of elegance and efficiency. In a boundary universe, mathematics neither is nor seeks to be value-free because its logical coherence depends on its instrumental usefulness and its transhistorical, even transcendental, truth-value. If cyberspace is the idealized projection of an underlying order—a working-out of the implications of boundary logic—its mathematical substructure reveals the coherence, not of a material world, but of an "objective" realm of ideal forms: the philosophy of elegance and efficiency on which virtual technologies are based.

Although, as Heim contends, cyberspace may be "Platonism as a working product,"[47] it owes its conceptual foundations to Leibniz's monadology, a mathematically based philosophy that forges principles of identity between formal constructs and the intelligence that imagines them. The indebtedness of cyberspace to a Leibnizian model both structures and, in my mind, qualifies its aesthetic—and political—appeal. Heim traces the "erotic ontology" of cyberspace back to Leibniz's notion of a universal language as the basis for a "binary logic, disembodied and devoid of material content"; this language, a calculus of signs, depends, he argues, on "eras[ing] the distance between the signifiers and the signified, symbol and meaning."[48] By collapsing these distinctions, Leibniz can imagine a point of self-observation, the monad, which exists as a self-contained expression of desire, "an independent point of vital willpower," a "nonphysical, psychical [substance] whose forceful life is im-

---

46. Brian Rotman, "Toward a Semiotics of Mathematics," *Semiotica* 72 (1988): 5.

47. Heim, "Erotic Ontology" (above, n. 15), p. 68.

48. Ibid., pp. 68–69.

manent activity."[49] Monads do not interact; they are not different from each other, and this lack of difference allows them to escape the relational economies of representation. As self-present, self-observing expressions of purposeful activity, monads are the metaphysical forerunners of Spencer-Brown's mark, idealized avatars of the omniscient perspective of a supreme being. For Leibniz, then, each monad microcosmically contains and reproduces to itself, without noise, without remainder, the intentional structures of an overarching order. This order is, at once, perceptual and aesthetic; the monadology thus offers its formal constituents the prospect of sharing an omniscient perspective, what Meredith Bricken calls "the experience of meta-observation, or the timeless infinity of 'higher' levels of consciousness."[50] The monadology, in short, describes an autonomous existence of desire that escapes contingency, representation, and materiality.

Because the monadology offers a powerful metaphor for an idealized network of mathematical calculation without loss or confusion, it becomes the implicit structuring principle of Bricken's Losp deductive engine and of cyberspace more generally. In describing his computational logic, Bricken states that "strong parallelism means independent, asynchronous actions by autonomous nodes, with no concept of a global perspective. Global results emerge out of local actions."[51] As I have suggested, however, the results of these "local actions" in boundary philosophy are foreordained because global coherence is constituted by the isomorphic relationships between aesthetics and truth-value that lie at the heart of Western conceptions of mathematics: truth-values emerge in the Calculus of Indications as functions of axiomatic operations in a "simple space," an idealized and aesthetic realm, not as the results of actions in a material universe. But the truth-values of simple, or cyber, space, as Bricken implies, are neither simple nor static. The appeal of the monadology and of boundary logic is that they offer complex, multidimensional models of reality, images of a nonlinear, universal network that transcends traditional notions of causality and linear representation. The seductiveness of a monadological cyberspace, in this respect, lies in its celebration of local action and self-actualizing existence as the necessary, indeed only, bases for global "results."

49. Ibid., p. 71. See also Gottfried Wilhelm Leibniz, *Monadology,* ed. Nicholas Rescher (London: Routledge, 1991).

50. M. Bricken, *Calculus* (above, n. 19), p. [10].

51. W. Bricken, *Introduction* (above, n. 28), p. 24.

Cyberspace aestheticizes action and intention: it encodes a vision of transcendent collectivity. Its politics, then, are not bound to Platonic oppositions between mind and body, or between totalizing and "asynchronous" modes of action or existence. Rhetorically, at least, many proponents of cyberspace celebrate the self-organizing, dynamic principles of subaltern resistance to dominant modes of thought. When the Brickens emphasize the significance of local and intentional action, for example, they edge toward a vocabulary reminiscent of those feminist critics, such as Donna Haraway, who advocate "critical knowledges sustaining the possibility of webs of connections called solidarity in politics and shared conversations in epistemology."[52] Although monadological idealism and feminist theory share little in the way of epistemology, their odd rhetorical convergence can be explained if we recognize that cyberspace is a dynamic and complex idealization—one that offers the alluring fiction of limitless possibilities and connections—rather than a stale recasting of oppositional logic. But if its commitment to monadological models suggests that cyberspace is always in the process of recasting itself stochastically, its principles of self-organization remain mathematical, ahistorical.[53] Nothing emerges in the ongoing present of this latter-day monadology because, quite simply, the monad—intentional, existential, formal—by definition can have no history.

IV

Even as cyberspace celebrates monadological modes of self-organization, then, it reproduces a hierarchical structure of value that naturalizes its mathematicizing of reality; reinscribes notions of identity as inherently fractured and alienated; and, as the price one must pay to travel in its realms of gold, makes that individual a function of the flows of capital and information. To analyze this structure of value—to specify the relations among mathematics, identity, and capital—we need to turn to Goux. In *Symbolic Economies after Marx and Freud,* Goux extends Marx's account of the money form of value to the economies of identity, desire, and representation. Gold, says Marx, operates as a "general equivalent," a universal measure of value, that underwrites but remains distinct

52. Haraway, *Simians, Cyborgs, and Women* (above, n. 6), p. 191.

53. On the stochastic processes of "artificial life," processes that involve a rethinking of the philosophical premises of computation, see Manuel De Landa, "Virtual Environments and the Emergence of Synthetic Reason," *South Atlantic Quarterly* 92 (1993): 793–816.

from all monetary transactions. Similarly, according to Goux, the father in the symbolic economy of identity, the phallus in that of desire, and language in that of representation function as general equivalents; they are idealized as absolute, transcendent determinants of value that are always absent from, yet always must authorize, all forms of material exchange and negotiation.[54] Put simply, underlying and informing our conceptions of self is the nagging, often neurotic, sense that we should be coherent, consistent individuals—perfect reproductions of a symbolic whole, an unshakable authority, the Father. But none of us, even those of us who are fathers, can ever attain this imaginary condition of coherence: the difference between the father as general equivalent and the father, or mother, or offspring as flawed human being is what we call psychology—or what Goux, speaking more generally, terms "interposition": "the dialectic of history," he suggests, "is embedded within the production and reproduction of interposition—which automatically poses two terms, separated by the 'inter' of a third."[55]

In emphasizing the ineluctability of mediation, of interposition, Goux challenges the binary structures of thought—the geneaologies of value—that structure Western metaphysics. The Platonist assumptions of mathematics—that mathematical laws are both an instrument to interpret the universe and, if we could only specify enough of them, an absolute and true description of its fundamental structure—reproduce the geneaology of value he discusses: mathematics is an intellectual currency, the means to explore the relationship between its own forms of representation and the natural world it seeks to represent, and a general equivalent, a universal measure of coherence, truth, and order. More specifically, Goux's analysis suggests that the mathematical foundations of cyberspace, the dynamics of identity formation (or, according to Meredith Bricken, identity conservation), and the workings of capital as the constitutive metaphor of virtual reality reinscribe a logic of alienation, an irrevocable split between lived experience and the idealized, symbolic realm of general equivalents.

Monads, of course, cannot be divided; they have no bodies to split from their minds, no contradictory tensions to fragment their intentions, no windows onto other monads in the network, no possibility of dialogue. As psychic avatars of divine intentionality, they are Leibniz's solution to the fallen, noisy, imperfect realm of

54. Goux, *Symbolic Economies* (above, n. 9), pp. 10–11.

55. Ibid., p. 239.

representation, to the fractured existence that humans suffer because they lack the ability to observe themselves objectively. But despite the claims of Leibniz and his followers, the monadology is a system of representation; it does not express transcendent truth-values but, as we have seen, gives formal shape to a host of contingent values, to a worldview that has more to do with seventeenth-century theology than with the eternal present of self-observation. A notational system that claims it is getting at the essence of a "reality" that lies beneath or beyond representation, as Rotman argues, is only reproducing the processes by which its practitioners mystify to themselves and to others what they are doing.[56] Because monadologists claim that they can imagine transcending the ideology of representation, they are also able to deny or to resist what they see as its effects—the notion that we are alienated fundamentally from ourselves and from what we seek to represent, from a mystical self-presence. Following the logic of Leibniz and Spencer-Brown, then, contemporary proponents of cyberspace can imagine a realm of self-presence, of an electronically mediated monadology, only by projecting, implicitly or explicitly, a fundamental, irrevocable alienation onto existence in "real," material reality: each human being always and already exists in a state divided from her or himself and from others.

If cyberspace is the solution to the solipsism of being bound in and by the proprioceptive limitations of our bodies, then "real" reality (a favorite locution among programmers at the HIT Lab in Seattle) consequently must be devalued as an always imperfect state, subject to the thousand shocks that electronically unmediated flesh is heir to. Bodies are, at once, nonmonadological because they are open systems, yet hopelessly solipsistic, rooted to a single proprioceptive existence. Virtual Reality naturalizes this alienation from one's environment and from one's self as the primary condition of existence, the "origin" and "essence" of a technologically unmediated subjectivity. Put simply, alienation, projected onto already-existing languages and identities, is the enabling condition of cyberspace as a philosophical—and ideological—construct. Without this presupposition, cyberspace becomes something closer to radio or television, a technology that has mediated our experience for decades and had profound effects on our identities and our culture but that forces us to recognize that we have been the products as well as the producers of technologies ever since we

56. Rotman, "Toward a Semiotics" (above, n. 46), p. 30.

scrambled out of the trees and onto the savannahs of Africa mil-
lions of years ago.[57]

Given its ideational roots in a mathematical monadology, then,
cyberspace lacks a means to analyze the alienation, the ruptures,
that it would heal. Because of its investment in formal boundaries
between inside and outside, calling and crossing, it has no way to
treat the boundaries—the technological mediation—that separate
virtual and real realities, no way to explore the ideological consequences of the material bases of interposition, that is, of the hardware that makes Virtual Reality possible. In an important sense, the
oppositional logic that cyberspace assumes it also reinscribes, oddly
reducing virtual technologies to the status of a technical problem
to be solved rather than the site of radical interventions in the human subject. In this respect, cyberspace reproduces sets of linked
oppositions: the individual is either whole, self-observing, and self-
creating (the state and process of calling in cyberspace), or she is
fragmented, unaware of her "real" nature, and alienated (the state
and process of crossing from virtual into real reality). This oppositional logic inscribes a dynamic of power, a politics of desire. The
subject is empowered in cyberspace to mark, to create, to render
her desire productive; when she steps out of Virtual Reality, she is
without ready access to the creativity that defines her existence,
and experiences her desire as a profound lack. This opposition between Deleuzian and Lacanian models of desire, however, is less an
analytic of cyberspace than a description of contrasting states that
a latter-day monadology offers.

In an important sense, cyberspace produces what Don Ihde calls
the "doubled desire" of technology. In the Western tradition, he argues, technology presents itself as a crucial means to empower-
ment, to controlling nature, to improving the quality of life; technological knowledge, therefore, becomes an essential political
means to secure and maintain socioeconomic control over others
and over the environment. On the other hand, the promises that
technology offers—pleasure, plenty, and self-actualization—ironically render it transparent: the purpose of technology, in this regard, is to re-create an enhanced version of natural existence.[58] This
doubled desire, the desire to master technology so that it can give

---

57. On the constructive, interventionist role of technology in the development of
prehuman culture, see Marvin Harris, *Our Kind: Who We Are, Where We Came From,
and Where We Are Going* (New York: Harper and Row, 1989), esp. pp. 25–34.

58. Don Ihde, *Technology and the Lifeworld: From Garden to Earth* (Bloomington: Indiana University Press, 1990), pp. 75–76.

us forms of power and pleasure that transcend the conditions of their technological production, is the enabling myth of cyberspace. Cyberspace promises to take us beyond the interventions of technology—ironically, only by repressing those interventions, by effacing the technologies on which it depends. In this regard, cyberspace represents not a new conceptual leap, but a new strategy to overcome or sweep under the rug the self-alienating problems of our doubled desires.

V

If, as Woolley suggests, reality in the age of supercomputing has become the property of formal, abstract mathematics, then it makes sense that for the Brickens and others the subject can be figured as both the creator and the effect of flows of information.[59] But as David Brande argues in his essay in this collection, these information flows are not new; they reinscribe a logic of exchange, a logic that Marx identifies as basic to capitalism.[60] In cyberspace, the individual resolves the divisions within her nature only by allowing herself to become an effect of the technology that re-creates her. She becomes the object as well as the subject of her doubled desire, the site on and through which technology operates. The promise of cyberspace can be thought of as the freedom to create narratives of endless re-creation, but these narratives do not emerge existentially; they are conditioned by the embodied experience of an individual who, when she jacks into the matrix, finds herself in a material realm rather than a simple space, a realm constructed by elaborate and expensive technologies which, at the end of the twentieth century, require enormous amounts of technical knowledge and skill in order to be run for, not by, the individual.[61] The individual in cyberspace can construct her narratives of absolute creative control—the omniscience that Meredith Bricken invokes—only by buying into a logic that is based far less on Leibniz's monadology or on boundary mathematics (how many would-be cybernauts have heard of either?) than on a familiar, even naturalized, logic of exchange that underwrites the symbolic economies—of money, identity, desire, and representation—that we already inhabit. As I have argued elsewhere, the sublimate of capital—of exchange value—

59. Woolley, *Virtual Worlds* (above, n. 11) pp. 247–249, 254.

60. See David Brande, "The Business of Cyberpunk: Symbolic Economy and Ideology in William Gibson," this collection.

61. On the materiality of virtual technologies, see N. Katherine Hayles, "The Materiality of Informatics," *Configurations* 1 (1993): 147–170.

always has been (at least since the eighteenth century) the currency of efforts to redefine and to reconfigure conceptions of identity.[62] Our culture's capital and symbolic investment in Virtual Reality, in one respect, has as its rationale the reproduction of the subject's alienation as both the cause and effect of continuing interventions in her reconstruction. In Foucault's sense, this essentializing of alienation becomes the necessary product as well as the grounding assumption of cyberspace to justify ongoing socioeconomic and individual efforts to overcome that alienation.[63] If the Brickens and Benedikt are correct, imagine the effects of technologically calling and crossing into and out of cyberspace, the constant reproduction of a desire to become a monad that only virtual technologies can fulfill. What this process would do, as Gibson suggests in his Sprawl trilogy, is encourage individuals to internalize the conditions of production that already are naturalized within economies of displacement and exchange, within our doubled desire to inhabit, and profit from, a reality that is always and already being marketed for profit.

If descriptions of capital, information, and cyberspace are mutually constitutive metaphors, then we might say that the experience of Virtual Reality is intended to send us back to real reality with a heightened appreciation of the exploitability of our environment. Cyberspace is the ultimate capitalist fantasy because it promises to exploit our own desires as the inexhaustible material of consumption. In this respect, cyberspace must destabilize liberal humanist conceptions of identity in favor of postmodern, fragmented, and performative subjectivities to market itself as a means to transform this always unstable and always incomplete identity into a thoroughly efficient desiring machine.[64] The dream of cyberspace is the dream of infinite production. In imagining the self as a monadological desiring machine, cyberspace actualizes a capitalist logic of self and society that is always in a process of collapse, what Slavoj Žižek calls a "permanent revolutionizing of [their] own conditions of existence."[65] Like Goux, Žižek rereads Marx and Lacan to argue that this "permanent revolutionizing" of symbolic economies de-

62. Robert Markley, "'So Inexhaustible a Treasure of Gold': Defoe, Credit, and the Romance of the South Seas," *Eighteenth-Century Life* (forthcoming).

63. See particularly Michel Foucault, *The History of Sexuality: An Introduction,* trans. Robert Hurley (New York: Pantheon, 1978).

64. See Gilles Deleuze and Felix Guattari, *Anti-Oedipus: Capitalism and Schizophrenia* (Minneapolis: University of Minnesota Press, 1983).

65. Slavoj Žižek, *The Sublime Object of Ideology* (London: Verso, 1989), p. 52.

pends on the *form* of ideology (what Goux calls the geneaology of value) rather than its content. Reality, therefore, is structured by the form of neurosis, both psychological and social, so that, according to Žižek, the "symptom" of our alienation precedes and structures its "real" existence. More prosaically, you are not a coherent self disfigured or disabled by a neurotic symptom; rather, your symptom, your neurotic sense of inadequacy, is the grounds on which you erect a stable enough identity to get you through the day. Drawing on Žižek, then, I would argue that the fiction of cyberspace is the symptom that precedes and enables the development of virtual technologies, the warrant for Virtual Reality to market its interventions in physical and conceptual realities as a "return" to an always lost, previously inaccessible, coherent, and newly monadological self. The form of the symptom of electronically mediated existence—cyberspace—thus becomes a means to imagine conditions of infinite productivity, the limitless possibilities afforded by rendering subjectivity as an effect of always unstable, always reconstituting metaphors of information and exchange.

I find it significant, in this regard, that cyberspace has emerged as a dominant cultural trope concurrently with an uneven but widespread ecological awareness. Although virtual worlds and our ecologically precarious planet are often described by analogous metaphors of a profound, even mystical organicism, the paradigm of virtuality is antiecological in its celebrating of the infinite productivity promised by monadological desire. In an important sense, cyberspace, cloaked in the rhetoric of a hyperallogenic postindustrialism, is an escape from the consequences of a century and a half of an industrialism fueled by oil, coal, and gas. Drawing on the language of thermodynamics, Michel Serres maintains that all physical systems, and the means that we use to represent them, are imperfect, entropic: "we know of no system," he maintains, "that functions perfectly, that is to say, without losses, flights, wear and tear, errors, accidents, opacity—a system whose return is one for one, where the yield is maximal. . . . This distance from equality, from perfect agreement, is history."[66] Cyberspace, the latest incarnation of the eternal present of the monadology, is an attempt to deny or repress the interpenetrating histories of labor, economic investment, technological development, and the ecological wear and tear that results from a society still dependent on nonrenewable resources for its sources of energy and economic and political power.

66. Michel Serres, *The Parasite*, trans. Lawrence R. Schehr (Baltimore: Johns Hopkins University Press, 1982), pp. 12–13.

To take only one example of the repressive, self-mystifying notions of cyberspace, think of the metaphor of the "information superhighway" which currently dominates discussions of the politics
of information. Superhighways are the product of a post–World
War II boom in automobile production, federally funded works
projects, and massive investments of capital and labor. When they
were designed and built, they were, at least in theory, inexpensive,
energy-efficient, time-saving monuments to a mobile culture intent
on promoting the "freedom" of individuals to possess personal
means of transportation. But to travel on I-95 from Boston to At-
lanta (the Ur-link of Gibson's BAMA axis) is to recognize that superhighways come with enormous costs: the fossil fuel economics of
scarce resources, pollution, the neglect of mass transit, and envi-
ronmental degradation. The metaphor of the "information superhighway" erases the complex natural and political ecology of the
Interstate Highway system, not to mention the enormous costs required to maintain it. Obviously, fiber-optic telephone lines are not
made of concrete, they do not need to be plowed in winter or have
their potholes filled. But neither do they escape "wear and tear, errors, accidents, opacity." Bringing the country on-line does not entail paving over wetlands or worrying about the effects of the internal combustion engine on the atmosphere, but it also does nothing
to redistribute the power that comes with access to information or
to make physical resources any more renewable. The metaphor of
the information superhighway reveals a mentality that assumes it
can remake the world without paying much attention to consequences.

The popularity of this image also has a profoundly negative effect on politically engaged discussions of informatics. Like cyberspace, the information superhighway is presented as the natural,
even inevitable development of science and technology; its existence as an integral part of an imagined future encodes a narrative
logic that suggests we can extrapolate from present conditions future possibilities. To a great extent, cyberspace depends on a coherent history of evolutionary progress in software and hardware
technologies, progress that leads inexorably to revolutionary break-
throughs. In popular accounts of Virtual Reality, such as those of
Howard Rheingold and Benjamin Woolley, narratives of the
progress of virtuality detail specific discoveries and profile eccentric
personalities, yet progress itself is presented as a logic that transcends these individuals. In an important sense, these narratives of
the evolution of cyberspace reinscribe the presuppositions of the
monadology: however individualistic, even solipsistic, our actions

may be, they are networked into a formal whole, a symbolic totality. Cyberspace makes sense to us, then, because it is presented as the extension of a logic—a progressive narrative of history and modernity—deeply embedded within our conceptions of science.[67] To challenge the political implications of cyberspace is ultimately to challenge the bedrock assumption that it is somehow already here.

My analysis of the Laws of Form, of the monadology, and of the ideology of the form of value has been intended to question the notions that cyberspace is in the process of arriving and that it marks a qualitative leap in technologies capable of intervening in and restructuring human subjectivity. To ask what is on the other side of the computer screen is, in my mind, a crucial step in dissenting from this consensual hallucination. Behind the screen of my laptop lie silicon chips, a battery, microprocessors, and even what seem to be a few old-fashioned screws. It runs (now rather dated) software programs engineered originally in California and Utah. My access to the presumptive world behind the screen carries with it an effaced history of labor, of people building machines to design and to build even more sophisticated hardware and software. The imaginary realm of cyberspace—of the reproduction and satisfaction of endless desire—is a fantasy based on the denial of ecology and labor, a dream that is also an apology for the socioeconomic power to bring together sophisticated technologies.

The debate about the control of virtual technologies, sure to intensify in the twenty-first century, might begin with the recognition that the consent of the governed (or, more accurately, the consent of the micro-managed) is not a hallucination. If technology is going to continue to intervene in individuals, then individuals had better be prepared to intervene in and contest the seemingly bedrock values and assumptions that virtual technologies help to naturalize as timeless, inevitable, and beneficial. Ensuring access to virtual technologies for diagnostic medicine, for example, requires concerted political action on behalf of a single-payer health care system—of rethinking the capitalism/socialism opposition in terms of mutual responsibility—rather than panegyrics to the information superhighway. The entry codes for a reconfigured cyberspace, the contested realm of a postindustrial ecology, are labor and, more generally, citizenship in a society that recognizes there are no frictionless systems, no wear and tear without loss.

67. See Joseph Rouse, "Philosophy of Science and the Persistent Narratives of Modernity," *Studies in History and Philosophy of Science* 22 (1991), esp. pp. 157–161.

The Business of Cyberpunk:

Symbolic Economy and Ideology

in William Gibson

David Brande

It is immaterial what consciousness starts to do on its own

Karl Marx, *The German Ideology*

Ask your friendly Hosaka pocket computer for a five-minute précis on William Gibson's *Neuromancer,* and it will probably reference several treatments of cyberpunk's place within the canon of science fiction as well as commentaries on the novel's representations of the vexed human-machine interface and their damaging implications for the onto-epistemologies of humanism.[1] Leaving aside issues of genre, literary influence, and tradition, it is the latter critical focus on the human-machine interface in the novel that I will address here—specifically, its portrayal of the flows of capital and the ideological mechanisms that construct the posthumanist "cyborg" in the first place. Far from inhabiting a "postideological" universe, the cyborg is best understood as an effect of advanced capitalism's restructuring of modes and relations of production and its corresponding transformations in ideological reproduction. With some exceptions (including commentary by Pam Rosenthal, Andrew Ross, and Larry McCaffery[2]), critics often situate Gibson's work

1. William Gibson's "Sprawl Trilogy" consists of *Neuromancer* (New York: Ace Books, 1984), *Count Zero* (New York: Ace Books, 1986), and *Mona Lisa Overdrive* (Toronto: Bantam Books, 1988).

2. Larry McCaffery, ed., *Storming the Reality Studio* (Durham, N.C.: Duke University Press, 1991); Pam Rosenthal, "Jacked In: Fordism, Cyberpunk, Marxism," *Socialist Review* 21:1 (1991): 79–105; Andrew Ross, *Strange Weather: Culture, Science, and Technology in the Age of Limits* (London: Verso, 1991).

within the context of "postindustrialism" and occasionally praise it
for its depictions of "late capitalism," without defining these terms
or saying exactly how his work embodies or works through them.
While it is, perhaps, out of a healthy skepticism of "vulgar" base/
superstructure models of economics and culture that leftist critics
are wary of making deterministic claims about the connections between macroeconomic transformations and the appearance of the
cyborg, the social and economic conditions of the production of
cyborg life nonetheless remain to be articulated.[3] A reading of Gibson that is informed by an awareness of the historical processes of
capital's tendencies to crisis and modes of alleviating (or reschedul-
ing) these tendencies, and that locates technoscience within the
coercive laws of the market, suggests some of the conditions of cyborg existence and indicates the economic and ideological significance of the development of "cyberspace." Gibson's fiction, read in
this way, constructs a mirror of existing large-scale techno-social relations, providing the cultural critic with the means for critiquing
those relations.

What is required in such a reading, however, is *not* a simple appeal to an economic base; Gibson's cyborgs—such as Case, the
"console cowboy," and Molly, the "razor-girl"—are not mere reflections of underlying economic processes, however much they may
be conditioned by them and however little they look like "well-de-
veloped" fictional characters. The cyborg, as a trope for the dissolution of the Cartesian subject, is symptomatic of consistent and isomorphic shifts in all areas of socio-symbolic activity, all the "modes
of symbolization," in Jean-Joseph Goux's terms—economic, subjective, philosophical.[4] Gibson's significance, for my purposes, lies neither in his prose style (which revolutionized SF in the eighties), nor
in his description of humanity's disappearance into technology,
but in his novels' staging of the modes of symbolization characteristic of a technologically advanced capitalist society. If, as I suggest,

3. See Donna Haraway, "A Manifesto for Cyborgs: Science, Technology, and Socialist
Feminism in the 1980's," in *Coming to Terms*, ed. Elizabeth Weed (New York: Routledge, 1989), pp. 173–204. Haraway, as a socialist-feminist, makes the inaugural gesture in this direction when she places the cyborg in the related contexts of the "informatics of domination" and the "homework economy."

4. Goux's argument, in Jean-Joseph Goux, *Symbolic Economies after Marx and Freud*,
trans. Jennifer Curtiss Gage (Ithaca, N.Y.: Cornell University Press, 1990), is complex
and will be taken up later in more detail. He argues that there are "a growth pattern
and statute that regulate sociohistorical structuration as a whole," a "regulated
process of equivalents and substitutions which cuts across the separate registers of the
general social body" (pp. 25, 21).

the cyborg is the "consciousness" of the techno-capitalist dream, then a corollary claim can be made about Gibson's fiction: it is a dream of late-capitalist ideology. And, far from being reason for leftist critics to dismiss Gibson, this is what should draw our critical attention. As Slavoj Žižek argues, "The only way to break the power of our ideological dream is to confront the Real of our desire which announces itself in this dream."[5] Žižek suggests, after Lacan, that it is only in the dream that we approach real awakening, the Real of our desire. This, he says, is not an idea of generalized illusion; Lacan argues that there is always a hard kernel, a leftover that cannot be reduced to a universal play of illusory mirroring: *the only point at which we approach this hard kernel of the Real is indeed the dream. . . .* It was only in the dream that we approached the fantasy-framework which determines our activity, our mode of acting in reality itself."[6] What is at stake, then, is the analytical benefit of taking Gibson's work seriously as a nuanced register of the contemporary ideological requirements of capital. My intention, therefore, is threefold: to resituate existing criticism of the novel by way of a brief return to Marx; to show how Gibson's cyborg characters are, in Goux's terms, the "operational subjects" of a consistent "mode of symbolization" or "symbolic economy"; and to illustrate how both these cyborgs and their socio-spatial context, "cyberspace," constitute, in Žižek's terms, an ideological fantasy of crucial importance to advanced capitalist society.

The question of historical-economic context provides a frame for resituating criticism of Gibson's work. Gibson is often discussed in terms familiar to readers of Donna Haraway's now-classic essay "A Manifesto for Cyborgs," because the cyberpunk science fiction of the eighties typically constructs a future in which Haraway's arguments about the melding of technology and the "human" subject have become the incontrovertible facts of everyday existence. This is definitely not to say that the cyberpunk writers of the eighties necessarily share Haraway's progressive feminist political agenda, but rather that they construct worlds in which the "cyborg" is a crucial metaphor for the disappearance of the unified, organic human body into ever more complex relations with technology: silicon chip implants, prosthetic devices, and the modification of neural chemistry. Katherine Hayles, for instance, makes the connection between Gibson's fictional texts and Haraway's theorizing while discussing new scientific paradigms and the cultural forms

5. Slavoj Žižek, *The Sublime Object of Ideology* (London: Verso, 1989), p. 48.

6. Ibid., p. 47.

they both inhabit and produce. Hayles defines "cultural postmodernism" as a "denaturing process" and uses this metaphor to illuminate postmodernism's implications for the "human":

> When the essential components of human experience are denatured, they are not merely revealed as constructions. The human subject who stands as the putative source of experience is also deconstructed and then reconstructed in ways that fundamentally alter what it means to be human. The postmodern anticipates and implies the posthuman.[7]

The denaturing processes of science and technology, as well as those of recent theory and cultural postmodernism, vacate the space carved out by and for Cartesian and Enlightenment versions of subjectivity, while they create multiple spaces for different forms of being—or rather, becoming—in the world, the (necessarily) variable forms of posthumanity, including the cyborg. Hayles's narrative links various cultural domains, showing how previously commonsense notions of language, space, time, and humanity are undergoing isomorphic changes within contemporary technoculture.

It is possible to contextualize Hayles's and Haraway's arguments by asking what motivates or at least conditions these transformations of cultural life. Without reducing language or subjectivity to superstructural reflections, it is still possible to see the processes of denaturation that Hayles discusses as being provoked by larger historical and economic processes. The denaturing of the subject is an effect of the historical-economic transformations described by Marx and Engels, in *The Communist Manifesto,* as characteristic of bourgeois socioeconomic life, a mode of social organization still with us, for all its recent mutations:

> The bourgeoisie cannot exist without constantly revolutionizing the instruments of production, and thereby the relations of production, and with them the whole relations of society. Conservation of the old modes of production in unaltered form was, on the contrary, the first condition of existence for all earlier industrial classes. Constant revolutionizing of production, uninterrupted disturbance of all social conditions, everlasting uncertainty and agitation distinguish the bourgeois epoch from all earlier ones. All fixed, fast frozen relations, with their train of ancient and venerable prejudices and opinions, are swept away, all new-formed ones become antiquated before they can ossify. All that is solid melts into air, all that is holy is profaned,

---

7. Katherine Hayles, *Chaos Bound: Orderly Disorder in Contemporary Literature and Science* (Ithaca, N.Y.: Cornell University Press, 1990), p. 266.

and man is at last compelled to face with sober senses his real conditions of life and his relations with his kind.[8]

I would argue that the denaturing of the "human" is the effect of yet another round of this revolutionizing of the modes and relations of production—not a fundamentally new kind of operation, but one consistent with the internal laws of the market that provoke it, especially in times of economic crisis. In *The German Ideology*, Marx argues that the production of consciousness—whether, I would suggest, it is conceived as unitary or as fragmented—is itself predicated upon a basic division of labor:

> Division of labor only becomes truly such from the moment when a division of material and mental labor appears. From this moment onwards consciousness can really flatter itself that it is something other than consciousness of existing practice, that it is really conceiving something without conceiving something real; from now on consciousness is in a position to emancipate itself from the world and proceed to the formation of "pure" theory, theology, philosophy, ethics, etc.[9]

Given the prior position of the division of labor, and the modes and relations of production to the formation of consciousness's conception of itself, the denaturing of the Cartesian subject and the articulation of cyborg or fragmented consciousness ought to be seen as an effect of changing modes and relations of production and of changes in the division of labor—a complicated effect, no doubt, with very different meanings for individual subjects: for some, at particular social strata, a relaxation of the distinction between manual and mental labor, and for others an intensification of that distinction through "deskilling," or the reduction of worker autonomy through automation.[10]

8. Robert C. Tucker, ed., *The Marx-Engels Reader* (New York: Norton, 1972), p. 388.

9. Ibid., p. 123.

10. See Gilles Deleuze and Felix Guattari, *A Thousand Plateaus: Capitalism and Schizophrenia*, trans. Brian Massumi (Minneapolis: University of Minnesota Press, 1987). They predicate subjectivity upon the division of labor when they argue that with the advent of cybernetic machines and increased automation, the process of "machinic enslavement," characteristic of ancient societies, is conjoined with the process of "social subjection," characteristic of the nation-state. In the former, "human beings themselves are constituent pieces of a [social] machine that they compose among themselves and with other things (animals, tools), under the control and direction of a higher unity" (p. 457). In the latter, more recent, form, "there is subjection when the higher unity constitutes the human being as a subject lined to a now exterior object, which can be an animal, a tool, or even a machine. The human being is no longer a component of the [social] machine but a worker, a user. He or she is subject-

Gibson's fiction, far from simply celebrating the conjunction of human and machine, locates its cyborg characters within the material contexts of the modes and relations of production. Looking, in Gibson, for some political agent—any sort of "revolutionary subject"—to oppose the regime of multinational corporate power, Andrew Ross complains that the novels ignore the great political movements of their time.[11] The rapidity of cultural change itself, however, the sense of a future that crowds the present, is one of the predominant themes of cyberpunk, which constructs characters who must *struggle* to make sense of this rapidly changing technocultural environment. That is, cyberpunk stages the "constant revolutionizing of production" and "uninterrupted disturbance of all social conditions" characteristic of its socioeconomic context. The Panther Moderns of *Neuromancer*, for instance, produce anxiety for Case, because he is unfamiliar with their sophisticated technologies of appearance and disappearance; with their "mimetic polycarbon" suits and extreme versions of plastic surgery, they symbolize both the revolutionizing of production and the disturbance of social conditions:

> The one who showed up at the loft door with a box of diskettes from the Finn was a soft-voiced boy called Angelo. His face was a simple graft grown on collagen and shark-cartilage polysaccharides, smooth and hideous. It was one of the nastiest pieces of elective surgery Case had ever seen. When Angelo smiled, revealing the razor-sharp canines of some large animal, Case was actually relieved. Toothbud transplants. He'd seen that before.
>
> "You can't let the little pricks generation-gap you," Molly said.[12]

The novel is less interested in specifying the political significance of these "nihilistic technofetishists"—that is, in locating their significance as political *agents*—than in instancing them as a symptom of the breakneck speed-up in cultural turnover time. After an academic on Case's computer screen explains their actions in terms of their neoterrorist self-consciousness and media savvy, Case, in a

ed *to* the machine and no longer enslaved *by* the machine" (p. 457). Under the regime of cybernetic capitalism, both forms of power are pushed to the extreme, "as two simultaneous parts that constantly reinforce and nourish each other" (p. 458). Thus, what appears to be a historical progression from the human to the posthuman is in effect a partial return to a prehumanist form of social organization. However, as Deleuze and Guattari might argue, the advent of the cyborg ought to be seen, not in terms of progression or regression, but as a "co-existence of becomings" in the service of the general axiomatic of capitalism, production for the market (p. 430).

11. Cf. the chapter "Cyberpunk in Boystown" in Ross, *Strange Weather* (n. 2, above).

12. Gibson, *Neuromancer* (n. 1, above), p. 59.

gesture the reader is implicitly invited to share, says, "Skip it."[13] Aside from conveying impatience with academic jargon, this passage introduces the third-person narrative account of Case's first encounter with the Moderns, in which Case locates them within a constantly mutating lineage of subcultures:

> Case met his first Modern two days after he'd screened the Hosaka's precis. The Moderns, he'd decided, were a contemporary version of the Big Scientists of his own late teens. There was a kind of ghostly teenage DNA at work in the Sprawl, something that carried the coded precepts of various short-lived subcults and replicated them at odd intervals.[14]

The point is not whether the Moderns correspond to the new social movements Ross wants to see represented; rather, it is how they embody the cultural manifestation of the laws of the market—specifically, the ever more rapid speed-up in turnover time—expressed here through "a ghostly teenage DNA." That Case, who has to bridge a "generation gap," is said to be only twenty-four illustrates the rate of mutation of this DNA.

Gibson's cyborgs, then, express the underlying market forces that condition their environment. The "constant revolutionizing of production" embodied by them necessitates speed-up in economic and cultural turnover time, which has the psychological effect of making time collapse in on itself. Istvan Csiscery-Ronay, Jr., captures this sense as it is narrativized in recent science fiction, including Gibson, Stanislaw Lem, and David Cronenberg's *Videodrome*.[15] Artfully casting this orientation toward the future in terms of a virus he calls "retro-futuristic chronosemiitis, or futuristic flu," he describes a narrative of the future that infects a host present and forecloses any sense of the present as a place in which an agent might choose its path into the future, a future that seems already on us and always just out of reach: "The retrofuture is an invention of our own age. It is unprecedented in earlier literature because the future has never before crowded into the present as much as now."[16] The danger of the retrofuture is that it responds to a "subjectless" feedback loop of technoscientific production, constructing it as already accomplished in the works of a present that has left

13. Ibid., p. 58.

14. Ibid.

15. Istvan Csiscery-Ronay, "Futuristic Flu, or, The Revenge of the Future," in *Fiction 2000: Cyberpunk and the Future of Narrative,* ed. George Slusser and Tom Shippey (Athens: University of Georgia Press, 1992), pp. 26–45.

16. Ibid., p. 33.

care and value in the wake of "a hypertrophic technological rationality."[17] In his focus on literary and filmic manifestations of this
"flu," Csiscery-Ronay characterizes it as a tactical consideration in
the construction of narratives about the future, one with ethical
implications for the ways we conceive of the future and our relation to posterity. He concludes his essay with a section on possible
"antidotes" to this flu, invoking the possibility of a "feminist futur-
ism" and the focus in Gibson and Bruce Sterling's later work on female characters as "value-carrying agents." Aside from the problematic nature of this latter impulse, making the feminine the
"carrier" of value (in an almost Richardsonian twist on the long
history of traffic in women), there is no doubt that futurisms devoted to imagining congenial ways of living can provoke critical attention to the present as well as more imaginative thinking about the
future. Like Ross, Csiscery-Ronay would like to see more science fiction that does not appear to succumb to ugly social and technological determinisms, that creates spaces in which readers might feel
empowered as agents with some control over their future and some
care for posterity.

I would argue, however, that the aspects of Gibson's fiction that
for Csiscery-Ronay carry the virus of the retrofuture do the ethical,
"diagnostic" work of representing the market-driven speed-up in
production, circulation, and consumption characteristic of any
"healthy" (as opposed to depressed) capitalist regime. David Harvey, in *The Condition of Postmodernity*, discusses the fundamental
forces at work in the market, which, I would argue, produce the effects described by Csiscery-Ronay:

> How is it, then, that the "bourgeoisie cannot exist without constantly revo-
> lutionizing the instruments of production, and thereby the relations of pro-
> duction"? The answer Marx provides in *Capital* is both thorough and con-
> vincing. The "coercive laws" of market competition force all capitalists to seek
> out technological and organizational changes that will enhance their own
> profitability vis-à-vis the social average, thus entraining all capitalists in leap-
> frogging processes of innovation that reach their limit only under conditions
> of massive labour surpluses. . . . Capitalism is necessarily technologically dy-
> namic, not because of the mythologized capacities of the innovative entre-
> preneur (as Schumpeter was later to argue) but because of the coercive laws
> of competition and the conditions of class struggle endemic to capitalism.[18]

17. Ibid., p. 35.

18. David Harvey, *The Condition of Postmodernity: An Enquiry into the Origins of Cultural
Change* (Cambridge: Basil Blackwell, 1989), p. 105; and see idem, "Flexibility: Threat
or Opportunity?" *Socialist Review* 21:1 (1991): 65–79.

It is Marx's notion of the *constant*—and constantly accelerating—revolutionizing of the modes and relations of production that most succinctly explains the nature of the processes subsumed under the heading of "advanced capitalism." Raw materials and labor power are exploited ever more efficiently; ever more labor is transformed into the machinery of fixed capital or, now, commodified as software; financial markets expand and accelerate to produce fictitious capital in spirals of indebtedness; the present borrows on an uncanny future, which returns like a bad dream. "Retro-futuristic chronosemiitis" is more than an ethical problem for science fiction narrative: it is another name for the structural, constitutive forces at work in capitalist society. If capital's dynamism is not the glory of Schumpeter's entrepreneur, neither is it the shame of ambitious science fiction writers (or venal consumers). Early in the novel, Gibson describes an "outlaw zone" within a twenty-first-century city: "Night City was like a deranged experiment in social Darwinism, designed by a bored researcher who kept one thumb permanently on the fast-forward button." This image might well be read as metonymic of advanced capitalism itself, rather than as symptomatic of a particular socio-narrativitis. As a "deliberately unsupervised playground" of technology and trade, what is Night City but a new and improved, twenty-first-century "enterprise zone"?[19]

Csiscery-Ronay demonstrates his awareness of the ways in which market forces condition our views of the future when he notes that the technologies sold to us to improve our lives are

> driven by the imperatives of breakneck production and circulation of commodities and information, governed by forces we inspire and encourage but which also constrain our destiny, not only in deterrence and the prospect of high-tech wars but also in deskilling and manipulation of our desires. The narcissism of the futureless present is actually a disguise for a presently future, an uninhabitable world created out of the consequences of our bad bargains.[20]

This passage is an elegant ethical critique of the retrofuture's "bad bargains"; what is left unsaid is the degree to which the retrofuture itself is a structural imperative for capitalism. Aside from justifiable appeals to open-ended futurist narrative and critical attention to the social context of technology, the retrofuture of cyberpunk, as it is manifest in Gibson, ought to be seen in the context of market forces that do not simply *encourage* technoscientific development

19. Gibson, *Neuromancer* (n. 1, above), pp. 7, 11.

20. Csiscery-Ronay, "Futuristic Flu" (n. 15, above), p. 30.

and increased consumption, but actually *demand* them. Gibson's "hyperrealism" has less to do with flashy technology, or cyborgs, or even the global simulacrum of cyberspace than with its extrapolation of a world governed by the coercive laws of the market—the intractable forces described by Marx, the forces in which, partly, he foresaw the downfall of the bourgeoisie. If the "expropriation of the expropriators" has yet to come to pass, the forces that were to lead up to it are more viciously in play than they ever were. This is the hyperrealism of cyberpunk: not mere "dystopia" as one narrative strategy among others, but extrapolation from the fundamental laws of the market, with its accelerating revolutionizing of the modes and relations of production. The "dystopic" elements of Gibson's environments in fact represent the consequences of accelerated production—crises of overproduction and the resultant devaluation of labor and capital:

> The landscape of the northern Sprawl woke confused memories of childhood for Case, dead grass tufting the cracks in a canted slab of freeway concrete.
> The train began to decelerate ten kilometers from the airport. Case watched the sun rise on the landscape of childhood, on broken slag and the rusting shells of refineries.[21]

If this depiction of the radical devaluation of infrastructure, fixed capital, and childhood innocence offers no blueprint for change, I would argue that the ethical burden of the narrative lies not in the possibilities it constructs but in the vividness of its staging of a seemingly intractable logic of the market, one theorized by Marx more than a century before.

Generally speaking, then, Gibson's infection of "retro-futuristic chronosemiitis" dramatizes the governing economic laws of its late-capitalist environment. Jean-Joseph Goux, however, in *Symbolic Economies after Marx and Freud*, articulates formal connections among symbolic domains across the social field that will allow us to situate Gibson's characterizations and fictional environments more precisely. He argues that all of Western society's "symbolic economies" follow the logic of the general equivalent as analyzed by Marx: the circulation of commodities regulated by a single measure of value—the general equivalent—which, as Marx argues, is set apart from immediate use and from other commodities: "A commodity can only function as general equivalent because, and in so far as, all other commodities set it apart from themselves as equivalent."[22] The logic of the genesis of the general equivalent form al-

---

21. Gibson, *Neuromancer* (n. 1, above), p. 85.

22. Goux, *Symbolic Economies* (n. 4, above), p. 17.

ways proceeds toward abstraction and convention. For example, within the realm of commodities, gold has historically regulated exchange, providing a standard by which "value" is produced in the substitution or replacement of one commodity for another (and Goux, following Marx, argues that it is only in substitution or replacement that value is created). If gold itself no longer stands in strict relation to the forms of currency directly involved in exchange—if currency is no longer convertible into gold—this development is consistent with historical processes of abstraction in the transformations of the value-form: "Floating currencies and the banking system are in line with the abstract autonomization of the symbolic."[23] In the symbolic economies of subjects and objects— that is, in the realm of desire—the father and the phallus mediate and regulate exchange: "The phallus is the general equivalent of objects, and the father is the general equivalent of subjects, in the same way that gold is the general equivalent of products."[24] Within all these domains of substitution and exchange there is a structurally homologous development through stages corresponding to Marx's description of the genesis of the money form: the elementary form, the extended form, the generalized form, and the money form. In Freudian terms, this progression toward an abstract, or general, equivalent moves through the oral, anal, phallic, and genital stages.

The significance of this argument lies in its formal linkage of the. economic and the subjective; without positing a causal deterministic relation between the two, Goux illustrates their isomorphisms. Of particular interest in this context is his argument that "[m]ore than any other, modern society has divorced economic practices from their diffuse symbolic valences"; because currency involves a segregation of values, the "developed commercial relationship" is not intersubjective, but an exchange between abstract positions.[25] This segregation, the rift between intersubjective and economic relations, not only gives rise to the notion of an economic base in political-economic thought but also spurs a depreciation of meaning for economic relations, leaving subjects only an operational relation to symbolic substitution and exchange. The institution of the general equivalent in the various socio-symbolic domains alters the "symbolic" irrevocably: "The symbol may ultimately lose its 'depth,' its verticality: instead of being a sign of the unfathomable, it becomes a signifying articulation, a structure, a machine. What is

23. Ibid., p. 130.

24. Ibid., p. 24.

25. Ibid., pp. 122, 129.

repressed by such a signifying economy is the dimension of interiority."[26] Gibson's cyborg characters, I argue, embody the "abstract positions" of subjects within the "developed commercial relationship," making visible this transformation of the symbolic and its consequent repression of interiority.

Gibson's novels offer little of the kind of pleasure provided by the "realist" novel's construction of psychological depth; his heroes and heroines are, rather, the "operative subjects" described by Goux.[27] Molly, the cyborg samurai in *Neuromancer* hired to aid in the emancipation of Wintermute (an artificial intelligence) from its electromagnetic shackles, characterizes her motivations as strictly "professional":

> "I'm an easy make." She smiled. "Anybody any good at what they do, that's what they *are*, right? You gotta jack, I gotta tussle."[28]

Both Molly and Case define themselves by their avenues of entry into extended circulation and exchange-value. For his part, Case, at the beginning of *Neuromancer*, is busy self-destructing, the result of his having been neurochemically maimed by previous employers from whom he had withheld stolen goods. He is no longer able to access the "bodiless exultation of cyberspace"; now, "Case knew that at some point he'd started to play a game with himself, a very ancient one that has no name, a final solitaire."[29] Apparently life outside the "matrix," for Case, is not worth living. While these characters' narrow self-definitions and lack of psychological depth could be taken as weak characterization, or as representations of the yuppie ethic of the eighties, I would suggest that Molly and Case make explicit the form of subjectivity conditioned by the triumph of exchange-value (under the aegis of the general equivalent) over other modes of symbolizing. Molly and Case are "denatured" in the sense that they fail to meet the expectations of a readership conditioned by modes of symbolizing characteristic of industrial capitalism and the cultural residues of earlier epochs.

Perhaps the most extreme example of the operative subject in Gibson is the character of the unimaginably wealthy Virek in *Count Zero*, who commissions the former art dealer Marly to find the maker of certain art-objects. Virek exists, biologically, within a linked system of "support vats" located somewhere outside Stock-

26. Ibid., pp. 131–132.

27. Ibid., p. 120.

28. Gibson, *Neuromancer* (n. 1, above), p. 50.

29. Ibid., pp. 6–7.

holm and is motivated by the search for "bio-soft," a new super-high-capacity medium for information storage and processing, which will allow him, he thinks, to escape his support vats for this more sophisticated and powerful material basis for consciousness. Virek is already something other than an individual human being; Marly's friend Andrea says: "If you believe the journalists, he's the single wealthiest individual, period. As rich as some zaibatsu. But there's the catch, really: is he an individual? In the sense that you are, or I am? No."[30] And to underscore the point, Virek's aide-de-camp, Paco, explains: "Señor is wealthy. Señor enjoys any number of means of manifestation."[31] Virek exists at the mobile center of the field of his wealth, which draws in art, people, technologies: "The Virek Collection, you see, is a sort of black hole. The unnatural density of my wealth drags irresistibly at the rarest works of the human spirit. An autonomous process, and one I rarely take an interest in."[32] He is less a man than an author function, or better, a "capital function," authorizing and underwriting the "autonomous process" of the play of capital. But, as author/capital function, he merely makes explicit, in an extreme case, the condition of any subject constructed by and significantly engaged in the production and exchange of meaning or money in a late-capitalist symbolic economy. Contrary to the thinking of Andrea and Marly, the difference between them and Virek is one of degree, not kind. As David Porush suggests, "In our inevitable cyberpunk future it's not only the exceedingly rich who aren't remotely human anymore. Everyone, like the total population of Sterling's Schismatrix, is either mechanized or bioengineered into fatal otherness."[33]

I would qualify Porush's remark with a claim that bears the symptoms of retro-futuristic chronosemiitis: if our inevitable cyberpunk future is already upon us, as differently positioned members of late-capitalist societies, it is because the exigencies of late capitalism and its modes of symbolizing condition the production of subjectivity in ways that problematize conventional notions of identity and agency. From his point of view as a twenty-first-century Howard Hughes, Virek describes the constraints at work upon his own "self"-determination: "I imagine that a more fortunate man, or a poorer one, would have been allowed to die at least, or be cod-

30. Gibson, *Count Zero* (n. 1, above), p. 100.

31. Ibid., p. 106.

32. Ibid., pp. 14–15.

33. David Porush, "Frothing the Synaptic Bath: What Puts the Punk in Cyberpunk?" in Slusser and Shippey, *Fiction 2000* (n. 15, above), p. 251.

ed at the core of some bit of hardware. But I seem constrained, by a byzantine net of circumstance that requires, I understand, something like a tenth of my annual income." In this encounter, Marly realizes, "with an instinctive mammalian certainty, that the exceedingly rich [are] no longer even remotely human."[34] I would argue, however, that what Virek makes clear is that his difference from Marly does not take the form of a great divide but rather of the distinction between "upstream" and "downstream": with his degree of insertion into capital flows, Virek's subjectivity is pure connectivity and force, stripped of any remnant of religious or Enlightenment dimensions.[35]

Not only the characters themselves but also the relationships between them demonstrate that the "posthuman" can be conceptualized, following Goux, in terms of the repression of interiority. For Goux, the subject is predicated on phallic-paternal "interposition" between mother and child in the third or phallic stage of development (which corresponds in his framework to the third or "general equivalent" mode of symbolization); it is this *scission* that "produces ideality and organizing technicality."[36] Interiority is also a product of interposition: between mother and child, subject and

---

34. Gibson, *Count Zero* (n. 1, above), p. 16.

35. Virek's physical body, his corpus, bears an interesting relation to his symbolic-economic body, his corporation. (My thanks to Katherine Hayles for suggesting this thematic for discussing Virek.) A corporation is an artificial person, a group body given the legal status of an individual. The body, then, is both the material substrate for human life and a governing metaphor in juridical and political thought: the corpus is Nature, the real, the unitary. The corporation comes afterward as a simulacrum of the corpus, the corpus-in-effect; it is the "artificial person," culture, the many, and the symbolic. In one sense, Virek is frightening for Marly because his wealth has allowed for the transformation of his corpus into corporation—in a reversal of the proper order of legal representation, Virek "himself" has become an "artificial person," not in metaphor but in fact. Instead of the conventional process of the many banding together to incorporate, to gain the legal status of the "natural" individual, Virek the erstwhile individual has become the many and the artificial. He "embodies" a shockingly complete falling-away from the natural body. In another sense, though, Virek's "nature" is uncanny in that the distinction between his corpus and his corporation is all too vague. The latter infects the former, carries artifice into nature, the way the future infects the present in retrofuturistic narrative. As market forces condition the temporal practices of economic and cultural life, they import the modes and relations of production into the human body in ways that revolutionize our conception of that body, disturbing our sense of its organic unity. This is the apparent novelty of the cyborg, which appears less novel when seen in the context of the development of industrial and "postindustrial" capital, with its technologically dynamic conjunctions of body and machine.

36. Goux, *Symbolic Economies* (n. 4, above), p. 239.

object, and (after Engels) between a primal relation to nature and a relation that has passed through the historical processes of labor to a "new," thoroughly socialized, nature—the "negation of the negation" of the mother. The repression of interiority, then, or the transformation of the symbol from "sign of the unfathomable" to "signifying articulation," occurs in the transition from the third to the fourth stages, from the phallic and general equivalent stages to the genital and "money" stages. This transition is consistent with a historical progression toward abstraction and convention, and the money form—which sublimates the general equivalent (gold) into currency (inconvertible "gold-in-effect"), and which corresponds to the genital stage of development—is the mode of symbolizing embodied by the cyborg. The money form, the symbolico-economic habitat of the cyborg, gives rise to the "pure symbol" and the evacuation of the spaces of earlier stages of development: "The analysis of economic exchanges shows that the notion of the pure symbol, in the sense of a disaffected substitute that can be perfectly arbitrary, conventional, and unmotivated, emerges of its own accord from circulation and thus from the intensification of social exchanges."[37] Gibson illustrates this process of abstraction when he writes that "[i]t was difficult to transact legitimate business with cash in the Sprawl; in Japan it was already illegal."[38] The "money-less society"—society in which currency circulates in the form of dematerialized, digitized data—does not do without *currency*: as Goux argues, "*Money* is a subjective notion, connected with idea of wealth; *currency* is an objective concept relating to the social organization of economic exchanges."[39] A money-less society intensifies the abstraction inherent in the symbolization process. While money is libidinally invested as "wealth," currency circulates as a depersonalized, de-eroticized marker of exchange value divorced from extraeconomic contexts. Therefore, even though the final stage of economic value is referred to as the "money" stage, it is "currency" that is at issue, and it is the mode of symbolizing represented and enabled by currency that announces the appearance of the cyborg.

The movement from the phallic and general equivalent stages to the genital and money stages flattens the subject and "dis-affects" social exchange. This can be seen in the relationship between Case and his old mentor McCoy Pauley (aka "Dixie Flatline"), whose character exists in the novel only as a literal abstraction: this Oedi-

37. Ibid., p. 127.

38. Gibson, *Neuromancer* (n. 1, above), p. 6.

39. Goux, *Symbolic Economies* (n. 4, above), p. 30.

pal figure has died, but his memory and prodigious skills as a hacker and thief have been retained as copyrighted software by the entertainment conglomerate Sense/Net. (One of Case and Molly's first tasks is to steal "Dixie" from Sense/Net's vaults.) Dixie has, in effect, been killed off as tragedy and returned as farce.[40] Dixie's ambiguous ontological status parodies the notion of Oedipal conflict—or phallic-paternal interposition—as one of the primary modes of symbolizing (and producing) interiority. Early in the book, we find out that Case had "been trained by the best, by McCoy Pauley and Bobby Quine, legends in the biz."[41] This cliché description of Case's paternal initiation into the rites of data thievery is subverted within the novel itself in a sardonic exchange between Case and Dixie. We find that the latter, as mere software, has a tendency to overuse the stock phrases of his previous incarnation. At one point, Case asks Dixie if he can think of any reason not to "have a look at an AI in Berne" (the implication being that examining an artificial intelligence is dangerous, since it is likely to wield deadly "ICE," or "intrusion countermeasures electronics"); Dixie replies, "Not unless you got a morbid fear of death, no."[42] Later, ready to crack the AI Wintermute's defenses in the effort to free it to join with its counterpart, Case asks Dixie a similar question and gets a similar response:

> "Sure," the construct said, "unless you got a morbid fear of dying."
> "Sometimes you repeat yourself, man."
> "It's my nature."[43]

40. Cf. the opening paragraphs of Marx's essay "The Eighteenth Brumaire of Louis Bonaparte" (in Tucker, *Marx-Engels Reader* [n. 8, above], p. 437) in which he writes:

> Men make their own history, but not spontaneously, under conditions they have chosen themselves; rather on terms immediately existing, given and handed down to them. The tradition of countless dead generations is an incubus to the mind of the living. At the very times when they seem to be engaged in revolutionizing themselves and their circumstances, in creating something previously non-existent, at just such moments of revolutionary crisis they anxiously summon up spirits of the past.

The cyborg, subject of both hopeful and anxious debate in recent years, can be seen to have a historical context, even a genealogy, which locates it firmly within the lineage of the bourgeois Oedipal subject, notwithstanding its place within the intensified social relations that have begun to erode the material-symbolic basis for its Oedipal predecessor.

41. Gibson, *Neuromancer* (n. 1, above), p. 5.

42. Ibid., p. 115.

43. Ibid., p. 132.

This "return" of the father as farce stages the symbolic movement from general equivalent (gold, the phallus) to the money form of value (arbitrary signifier of credit, disaffected network of social exchange). In this brief exchange is revealed the ambiguous, ambivalent quality of the cyborg. On one hand, the father has been killed, reduced to a ROM construct of his former self, lessening the immediate severity of phallic-paternal interposition; this is the aspect of the cyborg that draws the cautious optimism of Haraway and others, who see in it the embodiment of new and potentially liberating relations to machine and animal life and even the promise of a new form of politics. These political relations can be achieved only through the death of the father, that is, outside the symbolic framework of immediate phallic interposition. On the other hand, in this exchange, the father's death is, in effect, the means of the Father's return—not in the "person" of Dixie Flatline, but rather in the entire socio-symbolic network of power that has enabled (and enforced) his new form of appearance.

Dixie's laugh, which "came through as something else, not laughter, but a stab of cold down Case's spine,"[44] shocks Case because it is an unpleasant reminder that this entity with whom he works in cyberspace more or less as with any other character (and who still does better work than Case) consists entirely of software, a set of coded responses to any given stimuli:

> "Wish you weren't so damn jolly today, man. That laugh of yours sort of gets me in the spine."
> "Too bad," the Flatline said. "Ol' dead man needs his laughs."[45]

Finally, though, in his desire to be erased as payment for his end of the deal, Dixie demonstrates a "humanity" equal to any shown by Case throughout the novel. That is, this dead man's death wish implies an *in*difference between Case's life and Dixie's "life" (or between Case's "life" and Dixie's "death"), subverting the distinction between the organic life of the unitary bourgeois subject and the simulated life of a software representation of personality. Dixie, even more than Molly and Case, embodies the abstract positionality of the operational subject; his very existence, copyrighted by Sense/Net, has been thoroughly and explicitly commodified—reduced to a principle of exchange, of pure iteration and reiteration. Dixie is the refined and abstracted "free" laborer, the "embodiment" of the logic of alienation.

44. Ibid., p. 106.

45. Ibid., p. 169.

If Gibson's characters operate less on principles of interiority than through modes of connectivity, it is because they are the products—on all levels—of a symbolic environment in which the theological symbol, which undergirds the interiority of the subject, has been superseded by algorithmic iteration. The loss of a sense of the miraculous and its replacement by the cool technoscientific connectivity of everyday life is illustrated when Case, driving through Istanbul with Molly, asks her about the Seraglio; she responds,

> "It was sort of a private whorehouse for the King," she said, getting out stretching. "Kept a lotta women there. Now it's a museum. Kinda like Finn's shop, all this stuff just jumbled in there, big diamonds, swords, the left hand of John the Baptist . . ."
> "Like a support vat?"
> "Nah. Dead. Got it inside this brass hand thing, little hatch on the side so the Christians could kiss it for luck."[46]

In another historical context, the relic would have linked the subject to the sublime; in this context, Case's question (apart from its comically stunning historical ignorance) reduces it to its imagined bio-technical functioning. It is denatured by its recontextualization within a late-capitalist symbolic economy. As Goux writes, the symbol as a "sign of the unfathomable" becomes the symbol as "a signifying articulation, a structure, a machine"; as the forces and relations of production continually are revolutionized, and as technoscientific production "irrupts into the [social] relations . . . of production"[47]—that is, into the construction of subjectivity and intersubjective relations—Gibson's characters embody the form of subjectivity this transformation produces.

It may well be that these characters exaggerate the disaffection of life in "postindustrial" societies, that people find ways, even within the hypercommodified life of the postmodern megalopolis, to construct value outside the networks of commodity circulation—that the modes of symbolizing that produce the interior life of bourgeois subjects are still operative and still underwrite various kinds of exchange across the social field. What is at stake, though, finally, in my reading of Gibson's cyborgs (and of his construction of cyberspace) is not the degree to which they reflect or represent "reality," but the degree to which they stage the ideological fantasy that structures reality. To put it differently, reading Gibson atten-

46. Ibid., p. 94.

47. Goux, *Symbolic Economies* (n. 4, above), p. 196.

tively does *not* mean dismissing the "ideologically driven" content of his fiction and revealing the totality of social relations obscured by the mystificatory force of his prose.[48] Rather, I would argue, reading Gibson ought to involve close attention to the structure of the fantasy he creates, because it is that fantasy that itself structures the social "totality." These two interpretive operations correspond to fundamentally opposing ways of conceptualizing ideology, succinctly contrasted by Žižek:

> in the predominant Marxist perspective the ideological gaze is a *partial* gaze overlooking the *totality* of social relations, whereas in the Lacanian perspective ideology rather designates *a totality set on effacing the traces of its own impossibility.* This difference corresponds to the one which distinguishes the Freudian from the Marxian notion of fetishism: in Marxism a fetish conceals the positive network of social relations, whereas in Freud a fetish conceals the lack ("castration") around which the symbolic network is articulated.[49]

In the Freudo-Lacanian perspective, then, to the degree that we claim to be "the subjects of a look which views the facts as they are, we remain throughout 'the consciousness of our ideological dream.' The only way to break the power of our ideological dream is to confront the Real of our desire which announces itself in this dream."[50] Žižek briefly exemplifies this kind of reading in an allusion to Kafka, in which he argues that far from "subjectively distort[ing]" the fate of the modern individual within modern bureaucracies in a kind of "fantasy-image of social reality," Kafka's universe is the *"mise en scène of the fantasy which is at work in the midst of social reality itself."*[51] That is, he argues, we all know that bureaucracies are not all-powerful, but our conduct is governed by an "objective," effective belief that they are. Thus, bureaucracy as an "impossible" totality functions on the basis of a constitutive fantasy, on which people act even if they do not "believe" in it on a theoretical level. Speaking of the everyday lives of individuals in commodity cultures, Žižek suggests, "They are fetishists in practice, not in theory."[52]

Similarly, what Gibson's characters "represent" is not the reality of subjectivity within late capitalism, but the fantasy that governs the production of that subjectivity—the "interpellation" of the cy-

48. Cf. Ross in "Cyberpunk in Boystown," in *Strange Weather* (n. 2, above).

49. Žižek, *Sublime Object of Ideology* (n. 5, above), p. 49.

50. Ibid., p. 48.

51. Ibid., p. 36.

52. Ibid., p. 31.

borg. The mode of symbolizing, in Goux's terms, of late capitalism, as it manifests itself in contemporary institutions and technologies, hails a new kind of subject, but it does not do this "spontaneously," as Marx might put it. The interpenetrating domains of "postmodernism" constitute an (impossible) ideological dream—of a socio-symbolic totality in which the logic of the money form has supplanted all other forms of symbolic exchange. The cyborg is simultaneously the consciousness of this dream and the form of interpellation proper to it. To read Gibson's depictions of late capitalism, and of the cyborgs that inhabit it, as narrowly mimetic of real social relations would be to miss the ideological "content" of his fiction, which, finally, is less the content of his depictions of late capitalism than the process of interpellating subjects to inhabit the world his fiction "depicts"—the staging of the fantasy of the cyborg. As Žižek argues, drawing a connection between the Freudian interpretation of dreams and the Marxian critique of the commodity form, it is not the latent content of the dream or the secret behind the commodity form (labor) that is the end of analysis, but the secrets of the forms themselves, the dream-work and the genesis of the commodity form.[53] In this context, it is Gibson's staging of the fantasy of the cyborg that is the ideological "dream-work" of his fiction. The question, then, is what unconscious desire is articulated in the "work" or form of dream.

This question, however, needs to be posed in the context of an analysis of historically specific conditions of production/reproduction, such as Rosenthal's articulation of cyberpunk fiction with the new corporate strategies referred to as "post-fordist."[54] Generally speaking, she argues that the affect of cyberpunk is mimetic of that produced by the real social relations of post-fordism:

> In contrast to the relatively stable integration of the work force into the industries of fordism, Post-Fordism, on the other hand, poses a whole new approach to time on and off the job: the hyped-up, insecure syncopations of workaholism and unemployment, the increasing employment of part-time and contract workers, and more layoffs as flexible transnationals decamp to

53. Ibid., pp. 14–15.

54. These phenomena are discussed by David Harvey in terms of "flexible accumulation" and by others as "New Times": see Stuart Hall and Martin Jacques, eds., *New Times: The Changing Face of Politics in the 1990s* (London: Verso, 1990). All these discussions represent efforts by Marxist thinkers to comes to terms with "postindustrialism" in ways that do not naturalize it as did the early postindustrial theorists (cf. Boris Frankel, *The Post-Industrial Utopians* [Madison: University of Wisconsin Press, 1987]).

avail themselves of cheaper labor overseas, or as they retrofit their plants with computerized automation technologies at home. What until fairly recently had seemed a reasonably self-evident positive dynamic within a well-defined arena now seems at best a set of mixed messages within an environment of shifting boundaries and rapidly transmutating rules. The ability to decode such messages—or, more likely, to accustom oneself to occupying such shifting epistemological terrain—engenders a jumpy kind of cool, the nonchalance of cyberpunk toward the bad new future that is upon us. This is also the cool of the post-industrial work situation.[55]

In general terms, the breakdown of the uneasy cooperation among big business, big labor, and big government characteristic of the postwar decades has produced a time of uncertainty and rapid change in cultural and economic life. The curious blend of paranoia and schizophrenia in Gibson—the sense of watching fragmented, "operational" subjects who are themselves watched by large corporate entities—is a result of this breakdown. As one of the British characters in *Mona Lisa Overdrive* says, "Christ, we've still got a *government* here. Not run by big companies. Well, not directly."[56] Roughly speaking, the decline of the state entails the serious illness of the rationalist citizen-subject, the uneven process of the latter's disappearance into the cyborg. It is possible to read Rosenthal's articulation of cyberpunk and post-fordism in other than mimetic terms, however. If the "jumpy kind of cool" of cyberpunk is "also the cool of the post-industrial work situation," it may be that the "ability to decode such messages," which "engenders" this cool, is in fact the ideological "content"—or rather, the *effect*—of cyberpunk; that is, it may be that the effect of cyberpunk is to "inform" the subject with this ability. The relation between cyberpunk and post-fordist economy is, in my mind, less mimetic than symbiotic or parasitic.[57]

To comprehend the ideological and symbolic-economic signifi-

55. Rosenthal, "Jacked In" (n. 2, above), p. 89.

56. Gibson, *Mona Lisa Overdrive* (n. 1, above), p. 218.

57. Frederic Jameson, in *Postmodernism, or, the Cultural Logic of Late Capitalism* (Durham, N.C: Duke University Press, 1991), makes a similar point in the context of a discussion of private/collective existence in "third-stage" capitalism: "one has not grasped the spirit and impulse of the imagination of the multinationals in postmodernism, which in new writing like cyberpunk determines an orgy of language and representation, an excess of representational consumption, if this heightened intensity is not grasped as sheer compensation, as a way of talking yourself into it and making, more than a virtue, a genuine pleasure and jouissance out of necessity, turning resignation into excitement and the baleful persistence of the past and its prose into a high and an addiction" (p. 321).

cance of Gibson's cyberspace and the cyborgs populating it, it is necessary to flesh out Rosenthal's description of post-fordism and its relation to cyberpunk. It should then become clearer to what degree cyberspace is an ideological fantasy answering to one of the most intractable (and most vital) contradictions of capitalism itself. David Harvey describes the various tactics of "flexible accumulation" developed by corporations since the crisis of 1973–1975—for example, the "reorganization of production techniques (such as the development of 'just-in-time' systems), financial restructuring, product innovation, and massive expansion into cultural and image production."[58] Far from representing the natural and beneficial evolution of capitalism from industrial to "postindustrial" forms, these changes in the economy are driven by the inherent crisis tendencies of the market and should be seen, as Harvey argues, in the context of capital's history of response to periodic crisis conditions of overaccumulation. Capital and the governments that exist to both regulate and facilitate its operations have a limited number of tactics available to them to forestall, reschedule, or ameliorate these crises of overaccumulation.[59]

Colonization of resources and markets—the investment of capital and labor in geographical expansion—is a classic response that absorbs excess capital and labor. This "spatial fix," in Harvey's terms, "entails the production of new spaces within which capitalist production can proceed (through infrastructural investments, for example), the growth of trade and direct investments, and the exploration of new possibilities for the exploitation of labour power"; for the purposes of my reading of Gibson, the salient point is Harvey's suggestion that "[i]f continual geographical expansion were a real possibility, there would be a relatively permanent solution to the over-accumulation problem."[60] That is, the limits of geographical expansion and the speed-up of turnover times in all areas of economic and cultural life necessitate the production of new territory, and Gibson's construction of cyberspace responds to the tendency toward crises of overaccumulation with a fantastic—

58. Harvey, "Flexibility" (n. 18, above), p. 67.

59. Drastic devaluation of capital and labor is one obvious and destructive avenue out of crisis. Gibson, as I have argued, vividly illustrates this devaluation, especially in *Neuromancer* and *Mona Lisa Overdrive*, in his descriptions of wasted industrial landscapes like "Dog Solitude," where Slick Henry externalizes his demons onto kinetic sculptures constructed from the detritus of deindustrialization. These creations were inspired by the work of Mark Pauline (Survival Research Laboratories). One could also stress Gibson's affinity with the industrial music of the eighties and its response to the failed promise of the postwar boom.

60. Harvey, *Condition of Postmodernity* (n. 18, above), p. 183.

although not entirely incredible—vision of limitless virtual space for market expansion. Gibson's "matrix" stages the revolutionary force of the global market, its capacity for the production of space that anticipates Gilles Deleuze and Felix Guattari's directive to make "maps" and not "tracings":[61] instead of retracing or representing a previously existing domain or territory, the forces of capital as demiurge, as producer of signs and domains, combine to map a new and open-ended domain of production, circulation, and consumption. In his construction of cyberspace, Gibson has not represented the "reality" of new information technologies. He has staged both the regime of symbolization that enables a techno-capitalist order to exist and—obliquely—the internal, structural contradictions that drive it toward constant revolutionizing of space.

That Gibson refers to the data thieves in his fiction as "console cowboys" does more than conjure up the image of the lone male protagonist of much American literature and film: it evokes the thematics of westward expansion and the frontier—the fantasy of limitless open spaces, frontier without end. When Case is healed of the damage done to him by his erstwhile employers, he is able to get back in the saddle and access this virtual frontier once again:

> And flowed, flowered for him, fluid neon origami trick, the unfolding of his distanceless home, his country, transparent 3D chessboard extending to infinity. Inner eye opening to the stepped scarlet pyramid of the Eastern Seaboard Fission Authority burning beyond the green cubes of Mitsubishi Bank of America, and high and very far away he saw the spiral arms of military systems, forever beyond his reach.[62]

If this thoroughly commodified space is not exactly the same as the nonvirtual spaces of nineteenth-century westward expansion, it has the advantage, so the story goes, of "extending" this commodification "to infinity." This extension to infinity of commodifiable space is overseen and warranted by "the spiral arms of military systems," an image that ironically connotes the distance and sublimity of stars in the old sky as well as the force of the cavalry behind the nonvirtual colonization of the West.

Gibson plays ironically with this thematics of space when he refers to the extinction of the horse in a global plague:

> "Hey, Christ," the Finn said, taking Case's arm, "looka that." He pointed. "It's a horse, man. You ever see a horse?"
>
> Case glanced at the embalmed animal and shook his head. It was dis-

---

61. Deleuze and Guattari, *Thousand Plateaus* (n. 10, above), p. 12.

62. Gibson, *Neuromancer* (n. 1, above), p. 52.

played on a sort of pedestal, near the entrance to a place that sold birds and monkeys. The thing's legs had been worn black and hairless by decades of passing hands. "Saw one in Maryland once," the Finn said, "and that was a good three years after the pandemic. There's Arabs still trying to code 'em up from the DNA, but they always croak."[63]

This reminder that the old wide-open spaces are no more does the ambivalent work of illustrating the ecological ravages caused by a market-driven society and asserting the necessity of new wide-open spaces. That is, given the foreclosure of the old West and the devaluation of its icons, Gibson has transferred the ideological work done by the myth of the old West onto the infinite country of cyberspace—from the cowboy on his horse to the hacker at his deck. This is more than the reproduction of particular gender roles, although that is a partial explanation of Gibson's male protagonists; at stake is the constitutive ideological fantasy of space that enables capitalist circulation to continue.[64]

If, as Žižek argues, "ideology . . . designates *a totality set on effacing the traces of its own impossibility,*" and if ideological fantasy is what structures real social relations, Gibson's fantasy of limitless space does the essential ideological work of constructing (cyborg) subjects who are invested in an "objective belief" in this space, who will structure their behavior as if this fantasy were true, whether or not they "believe" it theoretically.[65] It is necessary for capitalist subjects to act on the basis of this fantasy of open spaces, on the basis of a belief in future opportunity, just as it is necessary for them to act on the basis of commodity fetishism, even if they "know better." It is possible, then, to think of cyberspace as a "symptom": if the symptom is what organizes jouissance and is ultimately (in the terms of later Lacanian thought) the linchpin of the symbolic network, one could say that the fantasy of cyberspace is the jouissance of the cyborg.[66] This definition would help explain Case's suicidal behavior in the opening pages of the novel: cut off from the jouissance of his symptom, his symbolic universe crumbling, Case loves his (lost) symptom more than himself. It would also explain the intensity of his reaction to his first trip back to "his

---

63. Ibid., pp. 91–92.

64. When Ross writes, somewhat dismissively, that "[c]yberspace, and the globally wired, satellite media Net that is a permanent feature of the cyberpunk landscape, is the heady cartographic fantasy of the powerful," this statement may have more significance than he intends (*Strange Weather* [n. 2, above], p. 148).

65. Žižek, *Sublime Object of Ideology* (n. 5, above), pp. 49, 36.

66. Ibid., pp. 71–75.

distanceless home": "And somewhere he was laughing, in a white-painted loft, distant fingers caressing the deck, tears of release streaking his face."[67] The method of this "cure" has been, not the interpretation and dissolution of the symptom, but the symptom's restoration; that is, the restoration of Case's access to cyberspace restores to him the jouissance of his symptom, that which binds his enjoyment to the symbolic order.

On a larger scale, the symptomatic function of cyberspace as linchpin of the techno-capitalist symbolic can be illustrated in a passage that Fred Pfeil cites in his argument that the extreme "modeling" of "landscapes" in *Neuromancer* invalidates traditional concerns of plot and character:[68]

> Home.
>
> Home is BAMA, the Sprawl, the Boston-Atlanta Metropolitan Axis. Program a map to display frequency of data exchange, every thousand megabytes a single pixel on a very large screen. Manhattan and Atlanta burn solid white. They start to pulse, the rate of traffic threatening to overload your simulation. Your map is about to go nova. Cool it down. Up your scale. Each pixel a million megabytes. At a hundred million megabytes per second, you begin to make out certain blocks in midtown Manhattan, outlines of hundred-year-old industrial parks ringing the old core of Atlanta.[69]

As Pfeil argues, it is pointless to take this description as mere "mise-en-scène" against which a plot unravels, but I would suggest that it is something more than a highly modeled and modeling landscape.[70] It is less a view of the territory than a staging of the forces of "deterritorialization" and "reterritorialization" constitutive of a late-capitalist economic order. In this staging, the decoded flows of labor and capital—free, naked, or deterritorialized labor, and the abstract wealth wrung from that labor and whatever "material" it labors on—have become so rapid, turbulent, and interdependent that in order for the system to survive it must reterritorialize them onto an even more abstracted iconography.[71] The "frequency of

67. Gibson, *Neuromancer* (n. 1, above), p. 52.

68. Fred Pfeil, "These Disintegrations I'm Looking Forward to: Science Fiction from New Wave to New Age," in *Another Tale to Tell: Politics and Narrative in Postmodern Culture* (London: Verso, 1990), pp. 83–94.

69. Gibson, *Neuromancer* (n. 1, above), p. 43.

70. Pfeil, "These Disintegrations" (n. 68, above), p. 87.

71. The "abstraction" of cyberspace, its reterritorialization of flows of labor and capital, could be conceived in terms of Bruno Latour's discussion of "centers of calculation" in *Science in Action: How to Follow Scientists and Engineers through Society* (Cam-

data exchange," of course, does not refer to the free exchange of ideas; rather, it has to do with capital circulation, the exchange of commodities.

Historically, capital has relied on the state for certain "compensatory reterritorializations"—that is, for certain regulatory paradigms or identities ("nation," the "people") to counterbalance the socially disruptive tendencies of the market, to provide rationalist or other "metasocial" guarantees within which the extraction of labor and circulation of capital can proceed more or less smoothly.[72] Harvey quotes from Deleuze and Guattari's *Anti-Oedipus* in discussing the shifting of the geographical bases of power:

> If space is indeed to be thought of as a system of "containers" of social power . . . , then it follows that the accumulation of capital is perpetually deconstructing that social power by re-shaping its geographical bases. Put the other way round, any struggle to reconstitute power relations is a struggle to reorganize their spatial bases. It is in this light that we can better understand "why capitalism is continually reterritorializing with one hand what it was deterritorializing with the other."[73]

Recently, as Harvey notes, there has been increased reliance by multinationals on governments for labor control to facilitate the spatial tactics of "flexible accumulation" or post-fordism; social

bridge, Mass.: Harvard University Press, 1987). Latour provides a paradigm for the analysis of the construction of facts in the context of science and technology, effectively explaining how a small group of people (scientists, engineers, administrators, managers) can exercise hegemonic influence over large populations. Briefly, Latour's study follows scientists and engineers as they go about constructing tactical alliances between human and nonhuman actants, weaving a network or a "cycle of accumulation" that "allows a point to become a center by acting at distance on many other points" (p. 222). Events, places, and people are, in Latour's terms, rendered mobile and stable as inscriptions (deterritorialized, decontextualized) so as to be brought back to a "center of calculation," where they will be combined in the form of further inscriptions (reterritorialized or recontextualized). The wider the cycle of accumulation, then the more inscriptions are brought back to the center, the harder the fact that is constructed (that is, the more expensive it is to refute), and the greater the capability for action at a distance, given—and this is an all-important given—correspondingly increased sophistication of labor at the center. "Abstract," then, is not an adjective describing a thought or a quality of mind; rather, it is a verb describing the particular labor practices within centers of calculation, through which large numbers of inscriptions are combined to form other more useful inscriptions. In the same way, in order for capitalists to realize surplus value from the circulation of commodities or the digital movements of currency, inscription techniques must keep pace with the intensification of these movements.

72. Deleuze and Guattari, *Thousand Plateaus* (n. 10, above), p. 455.

73. Harvey, *Condition of Postmodernity* (n. 18, above), p. 238.

control is one general example of the reterritorializations necessary to sustain capital flows. Gibson's matrix fulfills, at the level of ideological fantasy, the same structural function—enabling the realization of surplus value from the flows of deterritorialized data by rendering them intelligible and commodifiable. In *Mona Lisa Overdrive,* Gibson, in the character of Slick Henry, spells out the practical necessity for a reterritorialization of the increasingly complex informational flows characteristic of a late-capitalist order:

> People jacked in so they could hustle. Put the trodes on and they were out there, all the data in the world stacked up like one big neon city, so you could cruise around and have a kind of grip on it, visually anyway, because if you didn't, it was too complicated, trying to find your way to a particular piece of data you needed. Iconics, Gentry called that.[74]

As for the petty data thief, so for Virek or Sense/Net: the matrix is not only a grid of intelligibility allowing for data access and manipulation (a kind of exalted graphical user interface)—it is also both a new geography enabling the expansion of capital markets, ameliorating overaccumulation with a "spatial fix," and a domain of symbolic reterritorialization for the increasingly and bewilderingly complex flows of capital through those markets. Cyberspace is Gibson's fantastical geography of postnational capitalism, fulfilling the same basic functions as did the frontier and the nation-state in an earlier era: a fantasy of endless expansion of markets and future opportunity, and the means of a symbolic reterritorialization in the service of the greater deterritorializations of the global market.

If Gibson's "cyberspace" has become a synonym for virtual reality and information technologies, or if cyberpunk itself has become a cultural icon, this should not be taken as evidence of prescience or even extraordinary clear-sightedness; cyberpunk did not pierce the veils of ideology or work itself free from hidebound literary tradition to represent the world as it was actually becoming. Gibson's fiction is more complex in its relation to its cultural and historical-economic context. In the sense that it "represents" the culture of late capitalism, it stages the underlying market forces that drive that culture constantly and ever more rapidly to revolutionize its relations of production (part of the "cultural logic" of late capitalism, in Frederic Jameson's phrase). In the sense that Gibson's cyborg characters "represent" a new form of subjectivity, they embody new intensities in the degree to which the relations of production "intend" a new and inorganic body; they embody, too,

74. Gibson, *Mona Lisa Overdrive* (n. 1, above), p. 13.

the transsocial processes of abstraction that drive the interdependent domains of different symbolic economies within a consistent mode of symbolization. Finally, however, the distinction between representation and interpellation blurs. In staging the interdependent fantasies of cyborg and cyberspace, Gibson's fiction, on one hand, helps to structure real capitalist social relations by providing constitutive fantasies of the final subsumption of all symbolic exchange, and the subject itself, into the money form of value: cyberspace as the answer to crises of overaccumulation and the means to reterritorialize the deterritorialized flows of advanced capitalism. On the other hand, as an ideological dream, his fiction announces the lack that mobilizes these fantasies: the insatiable hunger of the market and its systemic and inevitable tendency toward crisis—the internal contradictions of capitalism, which are, paradoxically, the very source of its power. As Žižek writes, "the more it 'putrefies,' the more its immanent contradiction is aggravated, the more it must revolutionize itself to survive," and, therefore, "[f]ar from constricting, its limit is thus the very impetus of its development."[75] Gibson reminds us that behind the noisy, seemingly "radical" transformations in the world he constructs—apparently revolutionary changes in the body and in space—there is the "constant subliminal hum" of "biz."[76]

75. Žižek, *Sublime Object of Ideology* (n. 5, above), p. 52.

76. Gibson, *Neuromancer* (n. 1, above), p. 7.

Hacking the Brainstem:

Postmodern Metaphysics and

Stephenson's *Snow Crash*

David Porush

Metaphysics in Cyberspace

In William Gibson's 1984 novel *Neuromancer*, Case the barbarian hacker confronts Wintermute/Neuromancer, the new artificial intelligence he has helped to create, as a transcendent entity. "'So you God now? . . . You running the show?" he asks Wintermute. Wintermute doesn't deny it, he simply replies that he is now in contact with other beings like himself far out in the galaxy. The theme of meeting God in the computer is also taken up in other cybernetic fictions: In *Foucault's Pendulum* (1986), Umberto Eco's vision of Abulafia the transcendent computer is modeled on "routines" for cabalistic manipulation of the Hebrew alphabet (specifically, the letters of God's Name) intended by their thirteenth-century originator—Abraham Abulafia—to merge the "user" with Godhead. A. A. Attanasio's earlier SF novel *Radix* forcefully imagines a computer-god who goes mad after achieving divinity. In *Vineland* (1991), Thomas Pynchon portrays a cyborg device—the Puncutron Machine—providing a technologically assisted means to transcendent vision.[1]

Our centuries-long romance with technology, especially technologies for abstracting different faculties of the mind like language, the alphabet, mathematics, the telephone, and so on—produced by the urgent compulsion to exteriorize our nerve net, to

---

1. David Porush, "'Purring into Transcendence': Pynchon's Puncutron Machine," in *The Vineland Papers*, ed. Geoffrey Green, Donald J. Greiner, and Larry McCaffery (Normal, Ill.: Dalkey Archive Press, 1994), pp. 31–45.

achieve intimacy, to broaden the bandwidth of telepathic communications, to control and influence other minds—has already cyberspatialized us. This coevolution of human brain and communications tech has reached critical proportions in postmodernism, as we seem poised to leap across to some new cognitive-cultural state, heralded in near-apocalyptic imaginings about cyberspace and virtual reality. Yet, the emergence of metaphysical views on the postmodern literary scene is still surprising and represents a new turn, which this paper seeks to place in context.

The literature of cyberspace, a sheerly technological artifact, almost always envisions VR as giving rise to extrarational experiences and effects, including communication with metaphysical godhead. At the simplest level, mere transcendence in cyberspace may flow from the way cyberspace will reorient the mind to the experience of sensuous information BODILESSLY—that is, bypassing the normal route for sensuous experience and initiating it directly in that infinitely plastic sensorium, the brain/mind: that homuncular body without an organ. Cyberspace already transcends the physical "meat" body by creating a simulated "meta" body in the brain and communicating with it directly via electrical implants (the details of which are never explained, but which Stanford neurophysiologists are already beginning to explore)[2]—that is, in very literal terms, it is *meta-physical.* Cyborg hackers take the next evolutionary step that was begun in Daedalus's dream of flight to become electronic angels, freed from the laws of physics. For Jules Verne, new modes of transportation represented a conceptual breakthrough, as humans were liberated from their restrictive notions of their earthbound bodies in space and time. In the 1950s and 1960s, space

2. "For several months a group of electrical engineers and physicians at Stanford University has been able to tap directly into the electrical conversations of individual neurons in a rat's leg. Their listening device is a tiny microchip, designed to withstand the corrosive environment inside living tissue that they implanted between the severed ends of a bundle of nerves.

"The device itself is an impressive piece of engineering, but it is only a crude prototype of what the researchers eventually hope to develop: a computer chip that can be used to link an artificial hand directly to an amputee's nervous system, so that the hand can be controlled by the individual's brain, much as a natural hand is.

"When a chip was implanted between the severed ends of the rat's nerves, it not only survived inside the animal for 400 days, but individual regenerating nerve cells grew through the holes [they had drilled in the chip, which they called] . . . an artificial nervous system.

"The next hurdle: the design of the "active" chip that will use a radio transceiver to send and receive information between a rat's nervous system and an external data processor." (Sarah Williams, "Tapping into Nerve Conversations," *Science* 248 [May 4, 1990]: 555).

flight itself presented the vision of a new, paradigmatic relationship to the universe: "Space flight was the supreme myth of SF. Humanity, no longer Earthbound, would become somehow transcendent. The 50s and 60s were the romantic heyday of this myth."[3] But by the 1980s, with the poetics of the space program reduced to the pedestrian (golf on the moon) and mundane ("shuttle" flights in near-orbit), and with the explosion of cybernetic concerns in the culture, focusing particularly on the brain-computer link, a new mythology emerges. Gibson's striking descriptions of cyberspace in *Neuromancer* emphasize the "bodiless exultation" it gives the user, a soaring through metaspace, where the same mythology is reinscribed not in outer space but in Kantian inner space.

Still, SF and postmodernism here come into conflict on the issue of metaphysics. Postmodernism has traditionally—if it is not altogether too soon to talk about a "traditional postmodernism"— framed radical critiques of contemporary culture that reject essentializing viewpoints (other than the impossibility of an essential viewpoint). So it is a bit astonishing to survey postmodern cybernetic or cyberpunk fiction and find these metaphysical points of view expressed so frankly.

At the same time, postmodern fiction is also generally characterized by a critique of rationalism, and of the scientific/technological project of our culture in particular. Postmodern fictions resist rationalism with alternative epistemological methods that tend to focus on the irresolute and detotalizing aspects of language (paralleled in much of Derridean philosophy) while trying to capture the extrarational richness of experience. Kathy Acker, John Barth, Donald Barthelme, Samuel Beckett, William Burroughs, Italo Calvino, Robert Coover, Don Delillo, Umberto Eco, Joseph McElroy, Thomas Pynchon, and many others confront in their fiction the incompleteness and narrowness of science both thematically and in their deployment of literary styles—embracing discontinuity, ambiguity, paradox, metaphor, polysemy, cut-up and paste-back, collage, paronomasia (punning), and the phenomenology of silence—that contrast with the logical, unselfconscious, and factual discourse of science.

If we think, then, of postmodern thought generally as flowing from an underlying irrationalism or a skeptical, resistant critique of reason, especially of mechanics and reductive formalism and totalizing systems, it is not after all so surprising to find metaphysics emerging in postmodernism.

3. *Science Fiction Encyclopaedia*, ed. Peter Nicholls (London: Roxby Press, 1979), p. 595.

I argue in this paper that this turn toward transcendent and even metaphysical considerations evolves naturally from postmodernism's general irrationalism, its attempt to create a positive alternative to the rational and imperial discourses of science. Writ large, my concern here is with the persistently irrational, utopian, and metaphysical imaginations that are now being inscribed onto this still-mythical place called cyberspace. I suggest that these complexes of concerns, including the critique of rationality, seek resolution but rarely find it in postmodern fiction. I dub the resolution they seek Eudoxia. Finally, I reread the recent, second-generation cyberpunk novel *Snow Crash*, by Neal Stephenson. I examine how he formulates a transcendent viewpoint, only to reject the metaphysics it necessarily entails because his rationalism will not allow him to accept the consequences of his own vision. In reading *Snow Crash*, I propose that we can also see a reflection of our own academic reluctance to come to grips with an obvious metaphysical trend in postmodernism, perhaps because of our biases against metaphysics as an essentializing discourse.

Irrationality

Let us face facts: research into wetware implants in rats' nerves aside, in order to succeed as a full-bodied implementation, cyberspace technology must fully model the brain/mind so that we can induce in that brain/mind (in us) the illusion of proprioceptive coherence[4]—the illusion that there is a there there when "there is no there there," as William Gibson put it, or the illusion that our bodies are experiencing someplace they are not.[5] In other words, we are not going to get to cyberspace by assuming that all of nature is a vast, rational machine, because we will be dealing with that vast *ir*rational machine, the human brain. Even if we assume that the cybernetic apparatus for cyberspace linking will be merely a "rational platform" for human expression and telepathy, that machinery will still somehow have to find a medium, an interface, for the irrational effects of the human mind. So science must first describe the cognitive processes that underlie the massively irrational human behaviors based in the body. In short, to achieve cyberspace we must invent an irrational technology, a technology unlike anything we

4. This term was first brought to my attention by Don Byrd in his "Cyberspace and Proprioceptive Coherence," in which he traces the roots of cyberspace back to the Greek separation of the thing-in-itself from the idea-of-the-thing (Paper delivered at 2nd Annual Conference on Cyberspace, Santa Cruz, Calif., May 3, 1991).

5. William Gibson, *Neuromancer* (New York: Bantam, 1984), p. 270.

have today, a technology of the noncomputable that goes beyond the Boolean algebra of "either-or" and "if-then," and therefore beyond the limitations of any Turing Machine like the computer.[6]

Examining briefly the history of irrationalism reveals that the irrational has always been "pre-postmodern": a bastard, fugitive, monstrous, parricide concept, the ground for skeptical critique, part of an intellectual diaspora, an orphan ideal without a discipline to claim it. Investigating the irrational at its historical origin in Pythagorean geometry also unveils an interesting analog to cyberspace: it models how an irrational science can emerge from a rational (mathematical) technology (operation of numbers)—presaging, perhaps, how the irrational cognitive technology needed to build cyberspace might arise from our present-day impoverished AI models of the computer-brain.

The Pythagoreans of fifth-century Greece made an important distinction between counting and geometry. Counting was associated with commerce, imported to Greece from the Middle East by the Phoenicians; and it was obviously limited to integers (1, 2, 3, ...).[7] So the early Greek philosophers disdained counting, both because of its limitations and because of its commercial associations. In contrast was the mathematics of geometry, whose very name— "measuring the world"—implied a more global and even cosmological conception of the role of numbers. The world was made up of objects that were not all matched perfectly by the integers of counting. In order to measure distances accurately, you necessarily had to understand numbers that fell between integers—that is, fractions: 1/2, 1/3, 7/5, called the *rational* numbers because they were made by *ratios* of integers.[8] Nonetheless, Pythagorean mathe-

6. Turing Machines are limited to simulating only those behaviors that can be expressed as formal (mathematical logical) algorithms and in computable numbers. In *The Emperor's New Mind* (New York: Oxford University Press, 1989), Roger Penrose suggests that quantum mechanics, with its implication of consciousness in order to construct reality, requires a non-Boolean algebra or logic.

7. Since numbers are a re-presentation of the facts (Yanni has six [6] goats) which the mathematician can manipulate independently of those facts (if I bring four [4] more I will have ten [10] goats), there is already something implicitly hyperrealistic about numbers.

8. Furthermore, the Greek geometricians like Pythagoras had already embraced the idea of the point as a nonexistent entity, a locus in space having no dimensions of its own, and of the line as a representation of extension in space having no width or depth of its own. The drawing of a point by a dot on a piece of paper is only a crude representation of the pure geometrical *point*, and a line is a gross approximation or simulation of the ideal *line*.

matics was still anchored to—cast its shadows in—real and tangible manifestations in the world, however idealized the concepts of "line" and "point" were for the purposes of their logical manipulation. Geometry measured the dimensions of the earth and the objects on it. Numbers used in counting, the integers, measured *things*, discrete objects that could be held and owned.

To understand the breach in this philosophy introduced with irrational numbers, it helps to acknowledge the metaphysical dimension of Greek mathematics. The Pythagoreans were more like a secret guild or a religio-mystical cult than a scientific organization as we would understand it. They used the pentagram as a sort of coded signal—they named the sign "Health," or literally, "Salutation" (from the Latin *salus*, health)—to identify themselves to each other, and they used its name as their ritual, secret greeting. The influence of their mystical suppositions about the ideal shapes underpinning reality was very close to the surface of their pursuit of truth. They were ascetic vegetarians who owned their goods in common, employed purification rites, and believed in the transmigration and reincarnation of the soul. For them, manipulating numbers via proving statements about regular geometric forms was a means of communion with God's mind: "They proclaimed that true understanding of the world came through numbers, because all things in the world possess numbers."[9] So when one of the Pythagoreans, Hippasos the Akousmatic, stumbled upon the idea of $\sqrt{2}$ and the geometric proof that it was incommensurate with any integer or ratio between integers, the Pythagoreans suppressed it. In Book X of Euclid's *Elements*, a nearly contemporary commentator recounts the tale, which he received from Iamblichus of Hippus, that Hippasos was enticed onto a chartered cruise by his fellow Pythagoreans, but never arrived at his destination.[10] Whether the tale was true or not, this was effectively chilling, for the Greeks refused to use the method of commensurability for determining the values of numbers for almost eighty years for fear that someone would stumble on the incommensurable numbers (the irrationals), or that the Pythagoreans' secret society would punish them.[11]

The whole incident speaks to their commitment to the sort of idealism that later emerges in Platonic philosophy.[12] Numbers were

9. Ron Calinger, *History of Mathematics* (New York: Addison-Wesley, 1989), p. 30.

10. See George Johnston Allman, *Greek Geometry from Thales to Euclid* (Dublin: Hodges, Figgis, 1889), p. 43.

11. See Sir Thomas Heath, *A History of Greek Mathematics* (Oxford: Clarendon Press of Oxford University Press, 1921) vol. 1, p. 154.

12. Plato's own contribution to the philosophy of mathematics has been well docu-

the idealized root of reality, just as geometry was the idealized shape hidden behind all the worldy forms. For there to be a number for which no corresponding reality could be found was intolerable, blasphemous, heretical. It simply did not compute in their metaphysics, and thus was excluded from their rational system. Mathematics was not only abstruse, it required a metaphysical commitment to operate it properly and had little to do with "objective truth" as we understand it. (On the other hand, if the methods of modern science are bound up in metaphor and cosmological assumptions, then it too must have similarly furtive metaphysical commitments and also operates along orthodox—and therefore blind—avenues, which "reading" the metaphors of science will uncover.)

It remained for Eudoxos of Knidos, a shadowy but pivotal figure in the history of mathematics, to devise what now seems like a simple trick, though one with profound consequences: to sanitize irrational numbers, to make them salutory rather than salubrious. The effect of his work was to integrate geometrical manipulations of line segments in order to incorporate both the rational and irrational numbers into an acceptable theoretical system for determining the values of irrational numbers. From what we can reconstruct from accounts in Euclid's *Elements*,[13] Eudoxos apparently constructed the following *Gedanken*:

mented (see ibid., pp. 189 ff.). But ironically, the direct connection between Pythagorean cosmology and Platonic philosophy is through Eudoxos. Eudoxos created a "rational" theory of irrationals. After him, Theodorus uses Eudoxos's method to show the irrationality of $\sqrt{3}$, $\sqrt{5}$, on up to $\sqrt{17}$, and he is praised in Plato's *Theaetetus* for doing so. On the other hand, some historians claim that Eudoxos was already under the sway of Plato and the Socratic method when he formulated his greatest contributions to geometry (ca. 365 B.C.). In any event, it is clear the Eudoxos visited with Plato for about two months when at the height of his fame.

13. Actually, the following is a gross simplification of Eudoxos's method. An account similar to the one herein can be found in Steve J. Heim's excellent biography, *John von Neumann and Norbert Wiener: From Mathematics to the Technologies of Life and Death* (Cambridge, Mass.: MIT Press, 1980), pp. 58–77. But a far more accurate account of the method of proving incommensurability can be found in the histories of mathematics by Heath and Allman (above, nn. 11, 12) They describe a method by which a line is divided into two unequal parts but of whole measures (integers). By folding the smaller portion of the line back upon the larger and dividing the remainder of the line in the same proportions as the original, it can be determined that some measures have no integers as their root, but rather "never leave a magnitude which is too small to admit of further division, but that remainder is equally divisible ad infinitum." In Euclid's *Elements*, Book X, the commentator or "scholiast" adds the tale that "the first of these Pythagoreans who made public the investigation of these matters perished in a shipwreck" (Heath, *History*, p. 154).

Suppose that all the integers were mapped onto a line at equal spaces:

0	1	2	3	4	5	6	7	8	9 ...

Now map all the rational fractions that fall between them:

0 ...1/16 ...1/15 ...1/14 ...1/2 ... 2/3 ...3/4 ...4/5 ...18/20 ...78/99 ...475/511 ...1

Eudoxos's stroke of genius lay in asking a simple question: What numbers describe the points that lie between the rational numbers?

0   ...   4999/10,000   ...   1/2

By inverting the tenor and vehicle of his metaphor, and taking the line (rather than the numbers) as having a prior reality—the Map as having a priority over the Territory it is supposed to describe—Eudoxos opened a whole new, hitherto inconceivable, realm of abstraction, a hyperspace of irrationality founded on rational mathematics, much as the Internet is a communal experience founded on the machinery of communication, and the consensual hallucination of William Gibson's cyberspace is founded on the inexorable binary logic of computers. In other words, Eudoxos's achievement was not to discover irrational numbers but to create a world that could accommodate them, a physical theory of the irrational. In essence, he launched the entire possibility for an abstract mathematics, for it was the very lack of referentiality to real things that the Pythagoreans found unacceptable about irrational numbers.[14] It is hard to resist seeing a precursor of cyberspace in this Eudoxian turn.

The numbers between, because they described nothing the geometers could name, were called *alogos*, literally "wordless" or "indescribable." Ironically, when the Arabs preserved Greek learning through the medieval period, they translated the word as *surda*, which means, literally, "deaf" (i.e., unable to use words, or, again, wordless). The term finally emerges in English as "surd" meaning root (as in square root). It also gives us the word "absurd": the whole numbers that did not have integers or ratios of integers as their square roots were absurd. Even worse, as the Latin translation suggests, they were *irrational*, the term we have come to favor in contemporary mathematics, and which also conveys the deeper epistemological questions at the heart of Eudoxos's inversion. The unique suggestiveness of irrationals was such that Plato quipped in

14. ... although irrationals like pi (π) and *e* eventually emerge as having physical correlates and applications.

the Laws that "any man who was not aware of them was no smarter than a swine."

Voyage to Eudoxia: Cyborg Lit

Many intervening cultures have wrestled with the irrationality, the nameless absurdity, of these numbers that did not fit into idealized cosmologies and yet refused to go away. In fact, it is not until the nineteenth century that cosmology turns again to an appreciation for irrationals. Then, Richard Dedekind "invents" a theory of irrational numbers, but it is very similar to Eudoxos's. A few years later, Gregor Cantor takes them up again seriously, showing not only that Eudoxos was correct, but that the set of irrational numbers forms an infinity larger than that of the rational numbers.[15] Even in the twentieth century, enfolding the irrational into mathematics retains, however submerged, the aboriginal sense of foreboding that the Pythagoreans had.[16] What is the expense of this victory of abstraction? As the Pythagoreans were well aware, mathematics pursues a discourse of irrationality at the expense of literal referentiality, at the expense of relating the world to measurement, jeopardizing the intimacy between man and math.

So it is not surprising to find that early postmodernist literature sees the kindred relation between Hippasos's contamination of reason and the literary project. One of Samuel Beckett's enduring themes was the search for a suitable language to express that mental, inner realm of experience that lay beyond the rational, a language that did for the written text what irrationals did for mathematics. In Beckett's early novel *Murphy* (1938), we witness the early stages of his struggle with the problem, where he encounters the mathematization of the irrational as paradigmatic of the larger question of the discourse of irrationality. In fact, the novel is littered with puns, allusions, and references to the subject. In the first pages, the narrator tells us that Murphy went to sit at the feet of Neary, "a Pythagorean," who had learned the art of stopping his own heart: "For Murphy had such an irrational heart that no physician could get to the root of it."[17] This is signaled most clearly

15. Cantor's proof, which follows Eudoxos's own description, can be understood quite simply. Since, in geometry, the point is a dimensionless locus (having no breadth, width, or length, no extension), the sum of all the points on Eudoxus's line is infinite, but occupies no space. On the other hand, the irrational numbers, which occupy all the spaces between the points on lines by definition, are in sum a larger infinity.

16. Norbert Wiener, the father of cybernetics, earlier in his career had devised Wiener numbers as a rational way of dealing with irrational numbers.

17. Samuel Beckett, *Murphy* (1938; reissued New York: Grove Press, 1957), p. 3.

when we find a direct reference to Hippasos who is drowned in a mud puddle for revealing the incommensurability of side and diagonal.[18] (As usual, Beckett has slightly altered the image to suit his own obsessions—in this case, changing the ocean to the recurrent puddle.) Even the fact that each chapter begins with some precise mathematical, geometrical, or geographical fact and is followed by a wild blend of irrational human events speaks to this broader issue.

At one point in the novel, Murphy catalogues his inner life. There he discovers three mental zones, "light, half light, dark.":

> The third was dark, a flux of forms, a perpetual coming together and falling asunder of forms . . . [that contained] neither elements nor states, nothing but forms becoming and crumbling into the fragments of a new becoming, without love or hate or any intelligible principle of change. Here there was nothing but commotion and the pure forms of commotion. Here he was not free, but a mote in the dark of absolute freedom. He did not move, he was a point in the ceaseless unconditioned generation and passing away of line.
>
> Matrix of surds.[19]

The abstraction of this description itself could be taken to mean anything, but from its dynamic alocality, areferentiality, absolute freedom, and absolute absence of regularity, it is hard not to infer that Beckett is describing some elemental and seething state of the brain itself, much like the activity of the nervous system. We feel quite strongly that Murphy has been listening to his own nerve noise.[20] The point (so to speak) of the anecdote seems to be to circumscribe a realm where the irrational resides and then find a language to describe it. So we get such intensely disorienting metaphors as "he was a point in the ceaseless unconditioned generation and passing away of line. Matrix of surds," with its embedded reference to the origin of irrational numbers. Indeed, Beckett's project seems to be to simulate the irrational. In doing so, his artistic pro-

18. "But betray me," said Neary, "and you go the way of Hippasos."
"The Akousmatic, I presume," said Wylie. "His retribution slips my mind."
"Drowned in a puddle," said Neary, "for having divulged the incommensurability of side and diagonal."
"So perish all babblers," said Wylie.
"And the construction of the regular dodeca - hic- dodecahedreon," said Neary. "Excuse me." (ibid., pp. 47–48.)

19. Ibid., pp. 112–113.

20. Most who have spent time in an anechoic chamber report hearing a slight hum or buzz, which is actually the sound of their own brain activity.

ject parallels the major general aim of contemporary science, especially since the advent of the computer.

In the later work *Les dépeupleurs* (French original, 1954; published as *The Lost Ones* in 1973), Beckett resorts to a similar literary method: he circumscribes a realm where the irrational resides, and then shows the futility of trying to describe it in rational terms. Most of *The Lost Ones* is dedicated to ironically undermining a false-technical prose even as it tries to construct the imagination of a hellish cylinder-machine where four hundred naked bodies roam, each looking for its lost one.[21] In *The Lost Ones*, Beckett, too, alludes to Dante and to a metaphysical trapdoor in the ceiling.

The postmodern project takes its cue from the impossibility and potency of finding a satisfactory synthesis between the language of reason and the language of the irrational. Such a longed-for ideal, rarely consummated, I call "eudoxical discourse": the *eu doxia*, the good (transcendent) words or language, the linguistic parallel to Eudoxos's invention in numbers. Eudoxia is presently enacted in video games and cybernetic fiction, which will find their ultimate material marriage in the computer's cyberspace. Interactive and hypertextualized game spaces like Cosmic Osmo©®, Spelunx® (both from Broderbund Software), and "The Playroom©" (Borlund); interactive games on vast battlespaces played out among several users on the Internet; collaborative engineering of fiction by group processes using hypertextual bases like StorySpace (Eastgate Engineering) ; and primitive commercial playgrounds in cyberspace like those sponsored by Habitat®,[22] all augur this coming emergence of eudoxia. That they will rely on more and more potent simulations, which themselves will rely on a better understanding of complex mathematical forms like fractals and nonlinear partial differential equations now understood through chaos mathematics, is also inevitable. To make it happen, we will need a better and more robust model of cognition itself. It is obvious that the outcome will transcend the dialectic between literary representation and scientific epistemology. The early and tentative anticipations of this new order of discourse already indicate that it will collapse the multiple and inherently delusory boundaries between literature, cognition, epistemology, and science. It is this

21. See David Porush, *The Soft Machine: Cybernetic Fiction* (London: Methuen, 1985), chap. 6.

22. Originally developed by Lucasfilm for QuantumLink, an online service for Commodore 64 users. Club Caribe is its name now, supporting over 20,000 inhabitants, and up to 200 players at once. Habitat also exists in Japan on Fujitsu's NIftyServe, a Compuserve clone, supporting 2,000 players.

eudoxia that Italo Calvino describes in *Invisible Cities*, where one of his cities is Eudoxia, the site of a mise-en-abime reflexive simulation.[23]

For Giambattista Vico, the opposite of the rational is the *passionate*.[24] For most of our culture, the opposite of reason is *madness, poetry, faith,* or *metaphysics*. But as William Barrett notes in his study *Irrational Man*, the Greeks got to define the human as rational and rational meant logical—literally: *to zoon logikos,* "or even more literally, the animal who has language, since logic derives from the verb *legein*, which means to say, speak discourse. Man is the animal of connected logical discourse."[25] For my purposes, however, I prefer Gaston Bachelard's definition of the irrational. He associates it unremittingly with the *real*. For him, the great opposition is between rationality and *reality*, with rationality finding its best expression as science. This is a strange and wonderful inversion of our normal understanding of the term, but I think it reveals an essential truth. Most of us are accustomed to talking about irrational behavior as behavior that is not based on reality but is rather closer to madness. Yet if there is any virtue to the psychoanalytic revolution in our century, beyond its failure of method and its ultimately unpersuasive mythos about the sexes, it is the revelation that the ground of much behavior lies in irrationality. Bachelard writes:

> The assimilation of the irrational by reason never fails to bring about a reciprocal reorganization of the domain of rationality.[26]

> The epistemologist must therefore place himself at the crossroads between realism and rationalism. From this vantage he can grasp the new dynamism of those contradictory philosophies and study the dualistic processes whereby science simplifies the real and complicates the rational. The gap between explicated reality and applied thought is reduced.[27]

> In the face of this ramification of epistemology, is there any justification for continuing to speak of a remote, opaque, monolithic and irrational Reality? To do so is to overlook the fact that what science sees as real actually stands

23. David Porush, "Voyage to Eudoxia: The Emergence of a New Postrational Epistemology," *SubStance* 71/72 (1993): 38–49.

24. Giambattista Vico, *The New Science*, 3rd. ed. (1744), trans. Thomas Goddard Bergin and Max Harold Fisch (Ithaca, N.Y.: Cornell University Press, 1988).

25. William Barrett, *Irrational Man* (New York: Doubleday, 1958), p. 78.

26. Gaston Bachelard, *The New Scientific Spirit*, trans. Arthur Goldhammer (French original 1936; Boston: Beacon Press, 1984), p. 137.

27. Ibid., p. 10.

28 Ibid., pp. 8–9.

in a dialectical relationship with scientific reason. After centuries of dialogue between the World and the Spirit, mute experience is impossible.[28]

Though Bachelard is writing in the 1930s, he is anticipating many of the insights brought to critiques of reason by the existential phenomenology popular in European thought in the 1950s and expressed by Bakhtin, Heidegger, and Merleau-Ponty (and later by Feyerabend, Lakatos, and others). Bachelard's thesis is that the sciences are the source of epistemological innovation, not only in facts but in methods. Both facts and methods grow old and out-live their usefulness, so science is always in a position of innovating. Thus its strengths derive from intuition and induction, rather than deterministic positivism, empiricism, and deduction. His goal in *The New Scientific Spirit* was to sketch the shape of what he saw as an emergent "non-Cartesian epistemology" represented in "non-Euclidean geometry, non-Archimedean measures, non-Newtonian mechanics (associated with the name of Einstein), non-Maxwellian physics (associated with the name of Bohr) and noncommutative (or non-Pythagorean) arithmetic."[29] Thus, Bachelard's work provides the foundation for a fully irrational epistemology, one that is already expressed by literature and to which some contemporary sciences are tending. But that is another paper.[30]

For our purposes, Bachelard's salient point is that the opposite of science and rationalism is *realism*. Realism means acknowledging the unknowable complexity of natural phenomena—their "irrationality" including, presumably, their metaphysical properties—unmediated by instrumentalities or theories or models. And of all the slippery irrational phenomena out there in reality that we have attempted to define and replicate rationally, the slipperiest and most elusive is the brain/mind. That we can define the brain mechanically and merely rationally, when what it does best is quite irrational and irreducible, is the defining delusion of postmodern science and has become the informing debate of postmodernism generally. This delusion is also the predicate for cyberspace. We cannot emigrate to cyberspace until we accept the inherent irrationality of any model that can succeed in fooling our brain into thinking it is in an alternative space—the full delusion that we have been transported with all our sensory apparatus intact into an alternative reality, a technological designer drug where the hallucinations can be programmed and manipulated.

We are all programmed genetically to conceive of the world *as*

29. Ibid., p. 8.

30. David Porush, "The Anthropic Cosmological Principle and the Emergence of a Meaning Universe: Where Cybernetics, Literature, and Physics Meet," paper presented to the Conference of the Society for Literature and Science, Boston, April 1993.

if[31] a facility hardwired into human cognition.[32] Think about what
the brain does. In simplest terms, it takes physical impressions
from an irrational, inchoate reality and transmutes them into
thoughts, sensations, and the will to action. That is, it takes information from out there and translates it into meaning in here, in a
thoroughly different realm requiring a thoroughly different medium. At the risk of belaboring the obvious, the brain (not the mind,
but the physical organ the brain) is a metaphor machine, operating
continuously to carry meaning between realms that are in the larger sense thoroughly incommensurable.

The postmodern era is marked by the proliferation of this metaphorical nerve net, the exteriorization of the codes of metaphoresis
represented in the hard-wiring of the brain itself. So it is not surprising to find that romances of the brain, of cognition, and of cybernetics and cyborgs become *the* signal literature of postmodernism throughout the world. For instance, in a fascinating new
cybernetic fiction by the Japanese novelist Haruki Murakami, *Hard-
Boiled Wonderland or The End of the World*,[33] the hero discovers that
a brilliant but somewhat amoral scientist has implanted a circuit in
his brain. The circuit has three parts: one controls the id, one the li-
bido, and one the stable reality of the self. As the novel progresses,
the hero understands that the switches that keep these three circuits separate are dissolving and that his world will literally end, to
be supplanted by a dream- or nether-world (with which another
half of this complex cybernetic fiction is preoccupied). Though Murakami himself does not seem to realize it, he has phrased a neat
parable for the advent of virtual reality, a schema for the progress
of our cybernetic technologies, which exteriorize our imagination
to create a feedback loop between our brains, our tools, and our
culture until the loop is closed with tools that infect our imaginations.[34] In Murakami's story, when the last barriers between self and

31. Hans Vaihinger argues that the idea of "AS IF" is at the foundation of irrational
epistemology, in *The Philosophy of "AS IF": A System of the Theoretical, Practical and Religious Fictions of Mankind,* trans. C. K. Ogden (German original 1911; London: Routledge and Kegan Paul, 1924).

32. If, as I argue, this facility is cognitive, then it is hard to accept Jean Baudrillard's
claim in *Simulations*, trans. Paul Foss, Paul Patton, and Philip Beitchman (New York:
Semiotext(e),1983) that the hyperreal is a peculiarly postmodern condition.

33. Haruki Murakami, *Hard-Boiled Wonderland or The End of the World,* trans. Alfred
Birnbaum (Tokyo/New York/London: Kodansha International, 1991).

34. One cognitive scientist calls this "gene-culture coevolution": see Charles J. Lums-
den, "Gene-Culture Coevolution: Culture and Biology in a Darwinian Perspective," in
The Alphabet and the Brain, ed. Derrick de Kerckhove and Charles J. Lumsden (Berlin:
Springer-Verlag, 1988), pp. 17–42.

the world dissolve, with the aid of clever hardware, the world ends and reality's system crashes.

Murakami helps us to read postmodernism as that discourse documenting the (still thoroughly mythological) scenario that leads us to cyberspace: the frothing turbulence of the endocrine cascades bathing the synapses of our nerves, and the coaxial cables of the nerves themselves, exteriorize their contrasts onto our landscapes and civilizations, often at the expense of our peace of mind, sometimes to the profit of our arts, and finally, in a feedback appropriation of our perception itself—cyberspace.[35] So if there is anything new in postmodernism it is that the relationship between our minds and reality—the persistent delusion that leaps the bifurcation between sensation and thought—has now become self-evident, incarnated in hardware. We see that relationship obviously embodied in a prolific and ubiquitous technology, heralded with utopian fervor, that purposely mimics the mind: computers, communication devices, feedback controlling mechanisms, technologies for manipulating and exciting our own behaviors, techniques for manipulating genes and thereby reshaping human biological nature, and finally, VR. But the machinery has always been there tacitly, a necessary consequence of having a brain.

Cyberspace, then, is the metastasis of a brain condition. Call it a potentially happy cancer. Or better yet, a virus mutated from a genetic compulsion in the brain. It is the imperialism of a disciplined form of *as if* behavior. Cyberspace does not originate in—nor is it peculiar to—postmodernism, or even the twentieth century. Rather, the strong expression of this urge to exteriorize our own neurological drama can be found in any cultural moment when we confuse the metaphorical as the cognitive—or rather, *the moment when we recognize that the cognitive* is *the metaphorical.* This is my definition of transcendence.

Cyborg Utopias

Visions of utopia are usually isomorphisms—directly mapped projections—of our rational vision of human nature. How do you get to utopia? Model your view of human nature rationally and then invent a technology to control or direct that model—whether a political technology like the one Thomas Hobbes portrays in *Leviathan* (1651), a biological technology as in Aldous Huxley's

---

35. For a discussion of the interplay between nerves and hormonal bath in the creation of cconsciousness, see David Porush, "Frothing at the Synaptic Bath," in *Storming the Reality Studio: Essays on Cyberpunk and Virtual Reality*, ed. Larry McCaffery (Durham, N.C.: Duke University Press, 1992), pp. 331–333.

Brave New World (1949), a psychological technology as in B. F. Skinner's *Walden Two*, epistemo-technologies as in Francis Bacon's *New Atlantis*, information technologies as in George Orwell's *1984*, or just plain old technology generally, as in H. G. Wells's *Modern Utopia* (1905). I call these utopian visions "technologies" because they are deterministic decision procedures in all senses of that word: systems that seek and project perfect control. When the human is inserted into the utopian system, the result is a feedback loop in which the system encourages the "best" part and controls the "worst" part of human nature, while the human, in return, maintains the system with material, energy, information, flesh, and spirit.

In other words, the result of the inscription of a utopian vision onto a human is a cyborg: a natural organism linked for its survival and improvement to a cybernetic system. Even as early as the seventeenth century, Hobbes understood the essentially cyborg quality of utopia:

> [S]eeing [that] life is but a motion of limbs, the beginning whereof is in some principal part within, why may we not say that all automata (engines that move themselves by springs and wheels as doth a watch) have an artificial life? For what is the heart but a spring, and the nerves but so many strings; and the joints but so many wheels giving motion to the whole body such as was intended by the Artificer? Art goes yet further, imitating that rational and most excellent work of nature, man. For by art is created that great Leviathan called a Common wealth or a State which is but an artificial man, though of greater stature and strength.

This cyborg relationship between utopia and culture/human nature is not, I am convinced, an accident of a casually chosen metaphor or conceit. Rather, the pattern of utopian design as a feedback controlling machine is essential to the notion of utopianism. The model and program for controlling human nature rationally are always being revised in a feedback loop that cycles complexly among body, brain, mind, and culture, using language and images as the shared medium that influences all the components of the loop. As technology manipulates and alters human nature, and human nature adapts itself to the new technosphere, new versions of utopia arise, which in turn promote new technologies, which in turn change the context for defining human nature, and so on. Thus, every utopian inscription onto the human produces a new and improved vision of a cyborg. And the virtual reality–cyborg, the human plugged into a technology predicated on cognitive coherence giving out-of-body experience of the body, is what we seem to yearn for next.

The imminence of the cyborg is not a matter of speculation, it is a matter of reporting the news, a matter of postmodern sociology and introspection. We are already experiencing the reflux from a time twenty seconds into the future when our own media technologies will physically transcribe themselves onto our bodies, re-creating the human in their own images, forcing our evolution into the posthuman through a combination of mechanistic and genetic manipulations. We will all become texts in which the culture reads back to itself the computer codes inscribed on our bodies. The posthuman will be the governor—the *kybernetes* or pilot—in the inscription loop between the ultimate controlling technology of cybernetics (I call it "ultimate" because it defines the technology of selfhood, of mental identity of cognition, of the mind, of intelligence itself). Above all else a utopoid implies a vision of the world as perfectible. So we have heard and will undoubtedly continue to hear all sorts of utopoids about cyberspace: cyberspace will renovate human relations; it will unite art and technology; it will represent an altogether new and radical domain for improved social, psychic, and perceptual transactions. Bypassing the infirmities of the body, cyberspace will free the cripple and liberate the paralytic. Enabling multimedia and sensory access to the entire wealth of world data, cyberspace will deliver a universal education. Through its anonymity, cyberspace will invite the construction of a more ethical code and create norms for human interaction that strip distinctions of gender, class, race, and power. Cyberspace will provide a playspace for the imagination to roam free, liberating the mind from its inevitably neurotic relationship to the body. Cyberspace therefore has untold psychotherapeutic possibilities.[36] Yet cyberspace will incapacitate destructive urges and consequences by removing our bodies. Cyberspace will create the means for a pure and perfect democracy and universal suffrage in which everyone can vote immediately on any issue. Cyberspace will present the possibilities for "virtual communities."[37] Cyberspace will reconstruct the nature of the relationship between labor and time and labor and space and will reconstruct authoritarian technics as they are manifested in the workplace[38]—although one wonders who is

36. Kenneth Lee Diamond, "The Psychotherapeutic Possibilities of Cyberspace," paper presented to First Annual Conference on Cyberspace, Austin, Texas, May 1990.

37. Joseph Arthur Hunt, Ellen Putner Hunt, and Tony DeLeon, paper presented to First Annual Conference on Cyberspace, Austin, Texas, May 1990.

38. Pam Rosenthal, "Cyberspace: Utopian Workspaces in a Dystopian World," paper presented to Second Annual Conference on Cyberspace, Santa Cruz, Calif., May 1991.

going to empty the garbage and build the roads after we have all emigrated to this new virtual suburb. While cyberspace will undoubtedly present new opportunities for criminality, rape and physical assault will become impossible. Cyberspace will present a new opportunity for our manifest destiny, a new frontier.[39] Cyberspace will make war obsolete by turning it into a Desert Storm videogame.[40] Cyberspace will create a totalized hypertextual platform that will cure what ails American higher education.[41] We will become immortal there.[42] It will enable us to combine work and play in a new way. Even the music will be better there. Cyberspace will be the new, clean, virtual Eden to which we will all emigrate when this physical world becomes an unlivable ecodisaster. In cyberspace we will finally perfect the academic's dream of sex: we will be able to indulge lust without the involving of our bodies (perhaps I should have said "the dream of sex that's academic").[43] The New World, World Without End, amen.

How do we reconcile the rationalism of utopian vision with the obvious irrationalism of postmodernism generally, and of cyberpunk/cyberfiction in particular? Gibson's vision of cyberspace is dystopian, despite its desultory sensuality. How did American culture move so quickly from a postmodern vision of hell to a celebration of this technology not-yet-invented? It seems self-evident that utopian longings are part of a larger and more complex perception of massive change made imminent by a technological breakthrough. Every time culture succeeds in revolutionizing its cybernetic technologies, in massively widening the bandwidth of its thought-tech, it invites the creation of new gods. The invention of the phonological alphabet in the South Sinai in the fifteenth century B.C.E. almost certainly made the idea of an abstract monotheistic God thinkable for the first time. But along with such revolution comes inevitable apocalypticism, with its duality New World/End of the World. In other words, the utopianism of cyberspace predic-

39. Chip Morningstar, paper presented to Second Annual Conference on Cyberspace, Santa Cruz, Calif., May 1991.

40. James Der Derian, "Cyberwar, Videogames, and the New World Order," paper presented to Second Annual Conference on Cyberspace, Santa Cruz, Calif., May 1991.

41. I confess I'm responsible for this one: David Porush, "Toward the Hyperversity" (1990 Rensselaer internal memorandum).

42. N. Katherine Hayles, "Cyberspace and Immortality," paper presented at Eaton Conference, Riverside, Calif., 1992.

43. Jean Claude Guédon takes a somewhat more serious view of this in his presentation at the Second Annual Conference on Cyberspace, Santa Cruz, Calif., May 1991.

tions can only be understood as an attempt to tame, to rationalize, a more massively transcendent perception of metaphysical intrusion, the collision of the irrational future with the present.

Cyborg Metaphysics

Are these utopian predictions and prophesies founded on reasonable assumptions projected rationally, or are they expressions of deeper yearnings, apocalyptic urges that accompany any massive cultural change? The strong utopianism with which many are anticipating cyberspace, and the consistency with which cyberpunk fiction depicts transcendent or metaphysical occurrences there, suggest to me that cyberspace has become to our postmodern culture, with more than rational force, a sacramental architecture—even though it does not yet exist, quite. Like most sacramental architectures, cyberspace is prefigured as a site for the initiation or control of apocalyptism, where at some time in the future revelations from places beyond rational or material experience will occur.

Our postmodern, and presumably more sophisticated, view of cyberspace is hard to distinguish from romantic primitivism. Those who suggest that cyberspace is utopia are enacting an enduring, primordial, and probably compulsory form of cultural mysticism not much different from cargo cultists, whose towers of trash summon the airplane gods. Above, I considered how utopian wishes are already cyborgesque, transcribing notions of human perfection onto the memes, the cultural genetics that ultimately determine behavior. But within the loop of culture-body-brain-mind-language/images-behavior culture is a felt experience, and that felt experience includes transcendent and metaphysical events. As evidence, consider this passage written by an anthropologist who reads the ritual structure of a South American tribal culture as a computer program:

> One of the patterned aspects that now strikes me forcibly is the systematic manner in which certain ritual behaviors are replicated at various structural levels in the society, and certain concepts, expressed quite explicitly in Tzotzil, are replicated in various domains of their culture. It is as if the Zinacantecos have constructed a model for ritual behavior and for conceptualization of the natural and cultural world which functions like a kind of computer that prints out rules for appropriate behavior at each organizational level of the society and for the appropriate conceptualizing of the phenomena in the different domains of the cultures .[44]

44. Evan Z. Vogt, "Structural and Conceptual Replication in Zinacantan Culture," *American Anthropologist* 67 (1965): 342.

As among the Zinacantecos, this inscription loop embraces not just the rational technologies or academic speculations about them, but metaphysical perceptions and ritual forces in society that create the experience of transcendence, of communication with metaphysical entities or forces. Virtual reality or cyberspace is both a self-reflexive complex of discourses about redefining and reinscribing the human within a pure Cartesian space of mechanism,[45] and a New Jerusalem, a Promised Land for cargo-cult-like anticipations of transcendence. It has grown out of the very technologies that aim at modeling human nature—and manipulating it—through computational mechanisms, and yet, somewhat astonishingly, it is viewed by many as presenting not only utopian possibilities but transcendence itself.

In short, the intersection between the transcendent world and this one has always created or required an architecture that ultimately restructures society itself. Or better, perhaps we should say this: humans inevitably feel that a certain architecture is needed to summon the transcendent into this world. The reverse is also true: when the correct architecture is constructed, (we feel) the transcendent will be compelled to inhabit it willy-nilly: "Build it and they will come." For postmodernism, cyberspace is it. We are no more free of this metaphysical impulse than are the Zinacantecos.

The most interesting and poignant precursor of cyberspace as a sacramental architecture is found in the cultural revolution marked by the destruction of the Temple of Solomon in 70 A.D. and the subsequent rise of the Talmud that that destruction made possible. We can think of this as the evolution from a sacramental architecture to sacramental architexture. When the Jews are dispersed from Israel, they invent a portable structure that serves the sociological function of the Temple (that is, to define the Jews) but also creates a culture of interpretation that is highly hypertextual, interactive, open, skeptical, dialectic, and horizontal, paralleling the creation of a culture of diaspora. Contrast this to the fixities represented by a priesthood governing from a physical temple, interested in preserving fixed meanings of vertical and virtual authority. After the destruction of the Temple, the blueprint of the Temple, as well as its function, becomes literally enfolded into the structure of the Talmud.

---

45. See John Christie, "Of AIs and Others: William Gibson's Transit," in *Fiction 2000: Cyberpunk and the Future of Narrative*, ed. George Slusser and Thomas Shippey (Athens: University of Georgia Press, 1992), pp. 171–182. Don Byrd also makes this point in "Cyberspace and Proprioceptive Coherence" (above, n. 4).

Western culture marks the moment when it invents the architecture of the transcendent with a striking self-contradiction in the text of the Bible. This contradiction signals the moment that Western civilization turns from natural transcendentalism (recaptured by the post-Romantics) to an architectonic transcendentalism, of which cyberspace is the hypertropic expression. In Exodus we witness the Hebrews giving in to the human compulsion to create an architecture around the transcendent. In certain native cultures we see it in extreme rituals metastatized out of fearful pressure from encroaching technological civilization, like the cargo cults.

Exodus 20:20–22 takes a minimalist approach:

> Do not make of Me gods of silver, or gods of gold. An altar of earth shalt thou make unto Me. . . . In every place where I cause My name to be mentioned I will come unto thee and bless thee. And if thou make Me an altar of stone, thou shalt not build it of hewn stones; for if thou lift up thy tool upon it, thou hast profaned it. Neither shalt thou go up by steps unto Mine altar, that thy nakedness be uncovered.

The intention seems simple enough, here: "I can be worshipped anywhere. My altar must not rest on pillars or a base or be elevated so that you must get to it by ascending steps. A simple pile of unhewn stones resting on the raw earth is sufficient, and you can erect it anywhere." There is even a bit of joke to make the point: "Don't build Me any steps because as you ascend the steps, the congregation will be able to look up your robes at priestly private parts." However, it is only five brief chapters later, in Exodus 25–27, especially 27, that we read elaborate and mathematical specifications for the ark of the covenant, the repository for the tablets of stone on which were written the ten commandments. In all, there are nearly two dozen curtains, walls, veils, gates, doors, and containers that sanitize and protect the Holy of Holies from *"tamaid"*—the unclean in all its specifications, what Mary Douglas called "the abominations of Leviticus." What could be less in the spirit of the simple design for a portable altar a few chapters ago than this fetishistic elaboration of a blueprint for the Holy Sepulchre? There is also something unfortunate about it all, as we witness the institutionalization of an abstraction, a fearful attempt to surround the intangible with elaborate stagecraft. It might almost be taken for a return to idolatry, until we realize that it is idolatry turned inside out: an attempt to protect the mystery and intangibility of a central revelation, rather than to incarnate it in a graven image. Of course, this is not peculiar to Judaism. In fact, it is probably universal, with the exception of cultures that strictly forbid a sacramental sense of space, such as our own—unless you consider the shopping mall a form of sacramental space devoted to capitalism.

What *is* peculiar to Judaism, however, is the fetishism that persists around the text itself even though the Temple is destroyed and the Jews dispersed. This compulsion to create an architecture around the holy text becomes transformed, enfolded into the text itself, and ends up forming the central cohesive spirit of Judaism in the Diaspora, through the Middle Ages, and even into modern and postmodern philosophy.[46] Because there is no Temple, ritual sacrifice is abandoned—a ceremony that was inherited from nomadic days and elaborated upon in the architectural period. The hegemony of the priests is broken, a social and political development in its way as revolutionary as our modern democratic revolutions. The power moves from the priests, a class of men who rule by birthright and caste, to the rabbis, the poor graduate student types devoted to rewriting (literally) and reinscribing and interpreting the text of the laws. And finally, that political change paves the way for a monumental innovation. Instead of a literal, tangible architecture surrounding the Torah secreted in a sanctum sanctorum, the Jews evolve something much more portable, but more profoundly potent: an epistemology of interpretation, an architecture of hermeneutics that ultimately produces systems within systems of commentary that turn literal into metaphorical, and metaphorical into metametaphorical, and then back into literal again, in a twenty-century accretion of polysemous commentary, footnotes, marginalia, embroidery, folklore, interpretation, punning, numerology, and dialectic worthy of any postmodern hypertext, record of a noisy space-, time-, and genre-destroying symposium.

In short, the walls erected around the Holy Sepulchre in the Temple of Solomon evolve into the talmudical hypertext (see Fig. 1).

Interestingly, there is an extraordinary and unconscious relationship between the eventual shape of the page of the Talmud and the original blueprint for the Temple, with its concentric-rectilinear arrangement of spaces protecting an inner, unknowable core, a sanctum sanctorum protecting not a god or an idol, but a text whose central figure is a God whose name is unpronounceable, un-

---

46. See Susan Handelman, *Fragments of Redemption* (Bloomington: Indiana University Press, 1991); idem, *Slayers of Moses* (Albany: SUNY Press, 1982); Gillian Rose, *Judaism and Modernity* (Oxford: Blackwell, 1993); and idem, *Midrash and Literature* (New Haven: Yale University Press, 1989).

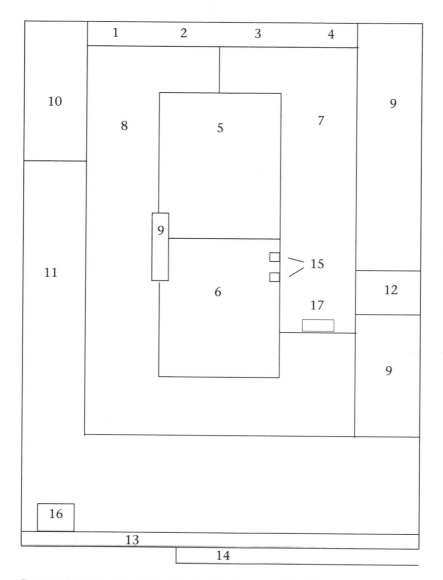

Figure 1. A typical page of the Talmud. Not all pages of the Talmud use all seventeen possible spaces set aside for different kinds of commentaries and footnotes. Each space represents a different kind of text: the central spaces are the original text, taken from the Books of Moses or other parts of the canon. The more central columns or spaces are reserved for ancient commentators. Small boxes usually refer the reader to other texts like hot-links in hypertext, sometimes within the Talmud itself. The earliest (physically most central) commentaries are by the Talmudic rabbis of the first through fourth centuries. The more marginal spaces reflect commentaries by medieval rabbis. The latest remarks are appended in the eighteenth and nineteenth centuries, although there is a recent edition of the Talmud compiled with new commentaries and illustrations by Adin Steinsaltz, so the exfoliating, antidoctrinaire, genre-destroying hyperspace of Talmudic discourse continues across the centuries.

utterable, and unwritable. But in translating physical space into the hyperspace of interpretation, the innovation of the Jews was to send out a new sort of invitation to transcendence: Come inhabit this world, not through the architectonics of material, but through a dynamic architecture of interpretation, dialogue, a never-ending symposium. The most portable altar of all is in your head and in your words. Midrash, commentary, or interpretation replace animal sacrifice and tithe-collection as attempts to communicate with the transcendent, a new model for the interface between the physical and metaphysical worlds, the architexture of the transcendent.

There is no doubt that both Temple and Talmud have at least one fundamental impulse in common: a fetishistic relationship to the text as holy object, summarized in the rabbinical injunction that many commentators both in and out of the religion believe is most basic to Judaism: *Build a fence around the Torah*. Where the Temple erects a fence in stone around the physical Torah, the Talmud erects a fence both in words and in an epistemology of interpretation whose fundamental tenet is that the name of God is unutterable, unpronounceable, and unknowable.

It may at first seem strange to suggest that this transformation from Temple to Talmud represents a precursor of cyberspace.[47] However, several writers, including Jacques Derrida himself, have located talmudic method as an important influence on postmodern alterity and resistance, at the level of writing, to totalizing knowledge.[48] And at least one postmodern author has groped after a similar connection between the Jewish method and cyberspace. Neal Stephenson in his cyberpunk novel *Snow Crash* (1992) analyzes the Judaic fetish to build a fence around the Torah as a form of what he calls "informational hygiene." He constructs a fascinating, comic, and apocalyptic mythology to explain why informational hygiene was necessary in the ancient world and how it made modern technology possible, and his novel depicts an apocalyptic drama in cyberspace and postmodern America based on that mythology. Stephenson's mythology gives us a basis for examining cyberspace's metaphysics.

47. My analysis was greeted as merely suggestive when I first delivered it in the form of a paper ("Transcendence at the Interface: The Architexture of Virtual Reality") at the 1991 Conference of the Society for Literature and Science, Montreal, Quebec, October 12, 1991.

48. Derrida's *Glas* (French orig. 1973) is a simultaneous critique of Hegel, particularly his anti-Semitism and totalizing philosophy, and an exploration, in two talmudically arranged columns, of postmodern literary style and thematics.

The Metaverse

Snow Crash is the latest in a line of essentially dystopian post-modern novels whose primary concern is the attempt to locate and define the human in an increasingly imperial cybernetic cultural space. It bears strong resemblance in theme and even in particulars of character and style to Thomas Pynchon's *Vineland* and William Gibson's trilogy (*Neuromancer, Count Zero* [1986], and *Mona Lisa Overdrive* [1989]). And it is the strongest of the cyberpunk novels since Gibson's work itself that attempt to express what pedestrian life would be like in a cyberspatial domain and how that virtual disembodied life would interact with "real" life.[49]

The novel is rich with intertwined themes, perspectives, and interpretations. Like many good postmodern texts it enfolds and collides a polyphony of voices and textual play, while keeping the paradigmatic postmodern themes of interpretation, ambiguous messages, cybernetics, cognition, and information at its center. It is in good measure both a satire and an adventure quest. Its style relies on creating a perceptual paradox through superfically slick surfaces intimating a hierophantic "beyond." However, my interest in it lies in the metaphysical history it provides for cyberspace, one that parallels my analysis above.

Snow Crash's narrative follows the intertwining trail of two itinerants: Hiro Protagonist, and Y.T. Hiro is a Japanese-American hacker living in L.A., and one of the originators of the cyberspace implementation—called here the "Metaverse"—that has become the world standard. He has gone freelance, though, which means that most of the time he is out of work. So he supports himself by delivering pizza. This makes him a sort of exemplary American (as well as a paradigmatic postmodern) hero, since, as Stephenson quips in the opening pages of the novel, by the turn of the century America excels at only four things: "music, movies, microcode and high-speed pizza delivery." Y.T. is a fifteen-year-old Kourier who travels on a hot-rodded supertech skateboard, "pooning" (harpooning) vehicles on the L.A. Freeway or merely drafting behind trucks in or-

49. I use the terms "embodied" and "disembodied" as shorthand. In fact, I feel strongly that the terms are misleading, since cyberspace will be phenomenologically indistinguishable from the experiences of our bodies in real space, which are always mediated by the mind/brain.

Interestingly enough, Gibson's most recent cyberpunk novel, *Virtual Light* (1993), seems to have been influenced strongly by Stephenson, who himself was evidently influenced by Gibson's earlier work.

der to get from point A to point B with her messages and packages. She is a female Mercury, whose name stands for "Yours Truly."

Economically, the country has collapsed into a series of franchises, run like capitalist shogunates by strong politico-cultural figures: Mr. Lee's Greater Hong Kong, Uncle Enzo's CosaNostra Pizza, Narcolombia, Reverend Wayne's Pearly Gates, and so on, forming a satirical portrait of alternative worlds worthy of Swift, colliding and sharing space on the postmodern platform. The Narcolombians are unredeemed murderers and their franchise promotes lawlessness. The CosaNostrans are cardboard Mafiosi and punks.

> "No surprises" is the motto of the franchise ghetto, its Good Housekeeping seal, subliminally blazoned on every sign and logo that make up the curves and grids of light that outline the Basin.
>
> The people of America, who live in the world's most surprising and terrible country, take comfort in that motto. Follow the loglo outwards, to where the growth is enfolded into the valleys and canyons, and you find the land of the refugees. They have fled from the true America, the America of atomic bombs, scalpings, hip-hops, chaos theory, cement overshoes, snake handlers, spree killers, space walks, buffalo jumps, drive-bys, cruise missiles, Sherman's March, gridlock, motorcycle gangs, and bungee jumping. They have parallel parked their bimbo boxes in identical, computer-designed Burbclave streetpatterns and secreted themselves in symmetrical sheetrock shitholes with vinyl floors and ill-fitting woodwork and no sidewalls, vast house farms out in the loglo wilderness, a culture medium for a medium culture.
>
> The only ones left in the city are the street people, feeding off debris; immigrants, thrown out like shrapnel from the destruction of the Asian powers; young bohos; and the technomedia priesthood of Mr. Lee's Greater Hong Kong. Young smart people like Da5id and Hiro take the risk of living in the city because they like stimulation and they know they can handle it.[50]

Hiro and his partners Da5id and Juanita have developed the basic software platform, graphics interface, and interactive rules for the Metaverse, and therefore they were also able to stake out the most valuable real estate site on the net for their stronghold. Readers fed on the more hallucinatory and enticing cyberspace conceived by Gibson might complain that Stephenson's version seems disappointingly pedestrian: the avatars (representatives) of real-world originals use simulacra of their real faces in the Metaverse. The geography uses more or less the same 3D orientation as real

---

50. Neal Stephenson, *Snow Crash* (New York: Bantam Books, 1992), p. 179. (Subsequent page numbers will be given in parentheses.)

space. Most of the activities of the net are devoted to capitalist exchange of data (what John Barth long ago called Informational-
ism[51]), infotainment, and just hanging out, so it is all not unlike
the virtual mall many of us fear it will be. And except for the ability
of avatars to experience extreme virtual speeds, even navigation in
the Metaverse lacks few of the soaring and transcendent actions
one might hope for or expect. Nonetheless, the Metaverse becomes
a site for intrigue as a very particular kind of devil enters this cybernetic garden.

Hiro and Y.T. get caught up fighting a conspiracy to sabotage the
net and control people's minds. The antagonist behind the conspiracy is L. Bob Rife, a fundamentalist mass-media preacher, a cross
between H. Ross Perot, L. Ron Hubbard, and Oral Roberts. The
means for this control, the titular Snow Crash, forms the central—
and for our purposes, most salient—premise of the novel. On the
streets, Snow Crash takes the form of a designer drug that induces a
type of aphasia, causing its users to babble in a glossolalia of basic
morphemes: "a ma la ge zen ba dam gal nun ka aria su su na an
da." The drug also causes an extraordinary susceptibility to suggestion and manipulation. In virtual reality, Snow Crash takes the
form of viral computer code that infects a host system merely by
revealing it "visually" to the avatar of the host. The results are
disastrous: the code sustaining the virtual avatar becomes infected,
causing the avatar to become inoperant and the brain of the host,
the live handler, to become infected as well, inducing the same
symptoms that the street drug does. It makes no difference whether
the victim sees it on the streets or through the medium of computer-driven VR goggles. If we consider virtual reality—the metaverse—and the real world (what Bruce Sterling called the "meat-
world") to be distinct realms, then Snow Crash breaks the barrier
between worlds. It opens a portal between the natural brain and its
artificial twin, the cybertech supporting the virtual world. In short,
it effects a transcendence of the categories *natural* and *artificial*, between the biological world and the simulated reality of cyberspace.
At least in this nonmetaphysical sense, the Snow Crash virus/drug
is a means to transcendence.

Yet, Stephenson's postmodern creation myth takes this physical
transcendence and makes it metaphysical. He rewrites the history
of the world, with special focus on the foundation of logocentric
Judaeo-Christian culture and the unique technology of the Word

51. In John Barth, *Giles Goat-Boy* (1966).

that it produced, a technology whose furthest extrapolation is cyberspace itself.[52] He also explores the ambiguous relationship between cyberspace—and the cognitive structures of the brain it must mirror in order to work—and irrationality.

Stephenson wrote *Snow Crash* partly under the sway of Edward Jayne's *Origins of Consciousness in the Breakdown of the Bicameral Mind*, first published in 1976.[53] In that book, Jayne theorizes that the most important events in the evolution of modern human consciousness can be traced to the sudden physical growth of complex connectedness across the corpus callosum approximately 10,000 years ago. When the two sides of the brain, left and right, started "talking to each other," humans suddenly achieved both self-awareness and the sense that there are other, superior or transcendent voices commanding them: the brain opened hailing frequencies to a sort of hierophony that humans naturally interpret as the voices of invisible beings or gods, the origin of religions and of the definitively human notion of transcendence.

Stephenson's scheme is predicated on this idea of having "two kinds of language in our heads" (presumably one for each cerebral hemisphere). All modern languages are acquired and tend to interact with the physical growth of the brain, so that languages can stamp their grammars or patterns on our brains as we learn them. But Stephenson, mixing his Jayne and Chomsky, suggests that there is also a tongue that is based in the deep structures of the brain that everyone shares. These structures consist of basic neural circuits that have to exist in order to allow our brains to acquire higher languages. Under the right conditions, we can access those parts of the brain, and when we do, we begin speaking in tongues, the basic morphemes that express the deep universal grammars all

52. In fact, one of the reasons Stephenson misunderstands the metaphysical implications of his own scheme is that he sees Judaeo-Christian culture as forming an evolutionary continuity. In fact, the hyphen does violence to history and the Judaeo-Christian label is misleading; the two cultural forms are dialectically opposed and mutually exclusive propositions, Judaism being opposed to myths of presence, which it resists by initiating a space-and-time-destroying loop of perpetual interpretations of text, and Christianity being essentially Christological, devoted to achieving the presence of Godhood through logos, the spoken word. For a longer discussion of this argument, read Jacques Derrida's *Glas* (French original 1973; English translation, Lincoln: University of Nebraska Press, 1987). Also see David Porush, *Illiteracy and Telepathy: Alphabetic Consciousness and Virtual Reality* (in preparation).

53. Edward Jayne, *The Origins of Consciousness in the Breakdown of the Bicameral Mind* (New York: Houghton-Mifflin, 1976). Stephenson reproduces drawings from that book and acknowledges it in his author's preface. For a sketchy critique of the theory see David Porush, "A Short History of Consciousness," *Omni*, October 1993, p. 64.

humans share. Thus, glossolalia—speaking in tongues—"is the output side of it, where the deep linguistic structures hook into our tongues and speak, bypassing all the higher, acquired languages":

> Under the right conditions, your ears—or eyes—can tie into deep structures, bypassing the higher language functions. Which is to say, someone who knows all the right words can speak words, or show you visual symbols, that go past all your defenses and sink right into your brainstem. Like a cracker who breaks into a computer system, bypasses all the security precautions, and plugs himself into the core, enabling him to exert absolute control over the machine. (p.369)

The name Snow Crash plays nicely on this combination of white noise ("snow") and a total system malfunction ("crash") of both software and fleshware. But this disease has an ancient origin. Civilization itself is first made possible with the collapse of the Tower of Babel. This is the signal event in human history, because before that time, all people spoke the same language, the Adamic language of transcendent grammar that expressed the patterns of the brain itself. This world was ruled by *me* sorcerers, wizards capable of programming other people's minds with verbal streams of data, little programs called *me*, parts of the oral tradition by which skills were transmitted and knowledge was secured. Stephenson compares these with viruses: bits of code that insinuate themselves into an operating system (the human brain) and then replicate themselves perfectly, forcing the system to do the work commanded in the invading code. With a nod toward AIDS and the HIV virus, Stephenson explains that any information system of sufficient complexity will inevitably become infected with viruses—"viruses generated from within itself" (p. 371).

But though the ancient Sumerian *me* system might evolve workable viruses or patterns of action from its own complexity, there was no room for *human* innovation in this perfect information game. So five thousand years ago the Sumerian equivalent of Prometheus, "a neurolinguistic hacker" named Enki, devised a piece of "software"—what the novel alternatively refers to as "medicine," a "metavirus," "countervirus," or a *"namshub"* —"to permit creativity and innovation, since viruses simply self-replicate and humans were acting as mindless hosts for the messages they contained. . . . [It] cut off the human brain from understanding the deep-structure language, the *me*" (p. 372).

The result of Enki's innovation was "Babel-Infocalypse." The world started babbling in mutually incomprehensible tongues that had to be acquired with labor and time. Furthermore, the old skills, like bread-making, were no longer automatic. Cut off from the *me* and from their deeper Adamic language, people had to devise their own technologies. In short, as one of the characters quips, "civilization began as an infection": "That's where the name Babel came from. Literally it means 'Gate of God.' It was the gate that allowed God to reach the human race. Babel is a gateway in our minds, a gateway that was opened by the namshub of Enki that broke us free . . . and gave us the ability to think—moved us from a materialistic world to a dualistic world, a binary world—with both a physical and a spiritual component" (p. 372).

Asherah, a cult of prostitutes, attempted to keep alive the old metavirus, through the exchange of bodily fluids that carry the herpes simplex virus, another echo of AIDS.

> Asherah is both a biological and a computer or informational virus. Herpes simplex heads straight for the nervous system and affects the brainstem. It's both biological and eventually mental . . . coiling around the brainstem like a serpent around a tree . . . brings the mother tongue closer to the surface, makes people more apt to speak in tongues and more susceptible to *me*. I would guess that it also tends to encourage irrational behavior, maybe lowers the victim's defenses to viral ideas. . . .
>
> We are all susceptible to the pull of viral ideas, like mass hysteria [and] . . . Bart Simpson t-shirts and bell bottoms jeans and Nazism. . . . No matter how smart we get, there is always this deep irrational part that makes us potential hosts for self-replicating information. . . . The only thing that keeps these things from taking over the world is the Babel factor—walls of mutual incomprehension that compartmentalize the human race and stop the spread of viruses. (p. 373)

This is where Judaism comes into Stephenson's metahistory. Judaism and its primary invention, the Torah, represented a successful countercult promoting "informational hygiene" and using a counter- or good virus, a namshub. Many Jewish sages themselves argue that one of the most fundamental tenets of Judaism is to "build a wall around the Torah," a *cordon sanitaire*;[54] and as we have seen above, liberating the Jewish religion from the priesthood and the literal architecture of the (Second) Temple of Solomon permitted the essential archite*x*ture, represented by the Talmud, to be expressed as both a rational and a metaphysical practice. This architexture was devoted to building open walls—permeable membranes—of polysemous interpretations, an ongoing process accret-

---

54. Marcel Proust's father, a Jew, invented the cordon sanitaire in Paris at the end of the nineteenth century.

ed over centuries and still promoted in Judaism, a living, evolving epistemological structure exfoliating from the omphalos of Torah. Stephenson considers that the Torah played a role in preserving civilization from Asherah, herpes, and the mind-controlling deep structures of the *me*. He teases out the story in a conversation between Hiro and the Hyperlibrarian Lagos, the intelligent but literal-minded interface to the vast database of the Metaverse. Lagos says,

> "Deuteronomy [the last of the five Books of Moses] is the only book of the Pentateuch that refers to a written Torah as comprising the divine will: 'And when he sits on the throne of his kingdom, he shall write for himself in a book a copy of this law, from that which is in charge of the Levitical priests; and it shall be with him, and he shall read in it all the days of his life, that he may learn to fear the Lord his God by keeping all the words of this law and these statutes, and doing them; . . . Deuteronomy 17:18–20.
>
> "So the deuteronomists codified the religion. Made it into an organized, self-propagating entity . . . I don't want to say virus. But . . . the Torah is like a virus. It uses the human brain as a host. The host—the human—makes copies of it. And more humans come to synagogue and read it.
>
> ". . . After the deuteronomists had reformed Judaism, instead of making sacrifices, the Jews went to synagogue and read the Book; if not for the deuteronomists, the world's monotheists would still be sacrificing animals and propagating their beliefs through the oral tradition."
>
> "Sharing needles," Hiro says.
>
> ". . . the Bible [is] . . . a benign virus. Like that used for vaccinations."
>
> "So the strict, book-based religion of the deuteronomists inoculated the Hebrews against the Asherah virus."
>
> "In combination with strict monogamy and other kosher practices," the Librarian says. "The previous religions, from Sumer up to Deuteronomy, are known as prerational. Judaisim was the first of the rational religions. As such, it was much less susceptible to viral infection because it was based on fixed, written records. This was the reason for the veneration of the Torah and the exacting care used when making new copies of it—informational hygiene."
>
> "What are we living in nowadays? The postrational era?" (p. 215)

This is a powerful rereading of Jewish evolution and its influence on the birth of civilization. It views the Torah and the religion that unfolds from it cybernetically, as a form of information practice designed to dampen the loop between cultural mutation or infection and the sorcery of oral preachment. What Stephenson does not go on to say is that alphabetic writing is the source of this power. And Judaism was the first religion to grow after the invention of the phonetic alphabetic in the Sinai or near Canaan in the fifteenth century B.C. Indeed, it grows a religion out of the essential unpronounceability (and unknowability) of the written name of God, the essential (and detotalizing) core of the Mosaic revelation and the central metaphysical tenet of Judaism.

Transcendence and the Postrational

Stephenson's fiction is both analysis and demonstration of this thesis: we are living in the postrational era. But I believe even Stephenson does not go far enough in exploring the implications regarding metaphysics that his fiction opens up, even though metaphysics is present in virtually every treatment of cyberspace. In one of the climactic scenes of the novel, Hiro tries to rescue Juanita, who has permitted L. Bob Rife to implant a radio antenna directly into her cortex, converting her into one of his robotic "wireheads." But it is clear she has somehow resisted the *me*, at the same time obtaining new powers to utter the *me* for her own ends. She explains to Hiro why she would flirt with the danger:

> "Don't you realize? This is it. This is the nerve center of a religion that is at once brand new and very ancient. Being here is like following Jesus or Mohammed around getting to observe the birth of a new faith."
>
> "But it's terrible. Rife is the Antichrist."
>
> "Of course he is but it's still interesting . . . . For a person who's interested in religion and hacking, this is the only place in the world to be." (pp. 401–402)

She reveals to Hiro that she now possesses the powers of the pre-Enki wizards: "I'm a ba'al shem. I can hack the brainstem."

In Jewish mystical tradition a "Ba'al Shem Tov" (literally: Possessor or Master of the Good Name) is an extremely righteous rabbi, someone possessing such deep penetration that he knows the unutterable name of God and can use it to control nature. Rabbi Judah Loew of Prague, the Medieval Maharal, for instance, was a Ba'al Shem Tov, who used his knowledge of cabalistic practice to create the Golem, the first cyborg.[55] Juanita has succeeded in finding the key to transcendence, finding the same creative trapdoor in the mind that Snow Crash effects in a disastrous way. She uses the cybernetic mechanics of language to hack the brain, to open hailing frequencies with spirits, angels, and gods.[56] But Hiro's reaction to

---

55. See Moshe Idel, *Golem: Jewish Magical and Mystical Traditions on the Artificial Anthropoid* (Albany: SUNY Press, 1990). For a cybernetic fiction about the theme of the golem see Marge Piercy, *He, She and It* (New York: Knopf, 1991), published in England as *Body of Glass* (London: Michael Joseph, 1992).

56. For a treatment of the neurophysiology of perceptions of transcendence, see David Porush, "Finding God in the Three-Pound Universe," *Omni*, October 1993, pp. 60 ff.

Juanita's metaphysics is parallel to the metaphysical implications of Stephenson's scheme: for both males, this woman's courtship with the mystical is beside the point.

I read this rejection of the metaphysical turn not as a lack of insight, but as the residual hold that one of the most potent viral ideas in our culture has on Stephenson and on his hero: a commitment to orthodox rationalism. In his autobiographical note appended to *Snow Crash*, Stephenson humorously describes himself as a hacker who spent more time coding for an abortive graphical precursor of the novel (to be implemented on a Macintosh) than he did writing it. He also says he "comes from a clan of rootless, itinerant hard science and engineering professionals...." He began his higher education as a physics major, then switched to geography when it appeared that this would enable him to "scam more free time on his university's mainframe computer" (from Postface, "About the Author").

The algebra of Stephenson's own mythology of liberal nomad rationalism demands that he acknowledges spiritualism as an activity just as important to civilization as word-tech. By his own recounting of the myth, "Enki broke us free . . . and gave us the ability to think—moved us from a materialistic world to a dualistic world, a binary world—with both a physical and a spiritual component" (p. 372). The effect of Babel/Infocalypse, of evolving out of the machine code and into natural language, of moving out of the Edenic prelogocentrism of direct mind control (programming code) and into the babble of uncertainty and invention, was to enlarge the domain of human activity in two directions at once. The first leads to words and languaging, which from thence forward *would never be enough*. The second leads to a recognition of the spirit world, a domain that transcends physical presence and mechanical activity, a realm beyond words, *which we can never utterly know*. In certain strong innovations of culture, like the invention of irrational numbers, or the enfolding of the Temple into the Talmud, or the utopian envisioning of cyberspace, it becomes clear that the tension between the word and spirit is the fundamental creative impulse in humanity. Civilization is always seeking to heal the rift, to bring the Word and the Spirit into perfect communion—one of the nostalgias that Derrida derides. Yet as I have argued, this yearning for a eudoxical discourse, where the map and the territory become one and help us transcend dualisms like rationality and irrationality, is at the heart of postmodern literature. And this yearning is indistinguishable from the desire for transcendence.

Yet, rather than pursue the implications of spiritualism, Stephenson emphasizes Judaism's rationality (following many historians of theology), both mistaking the meaning of the compulsion to erect a fence around the Torah and virtually disavowing the transcendent and metaphysical implications of his own mythos about it, or, for that matter, the spiritual technology represented in Talmud and cabala. The word "irrational" occurs once in the novel, as a disparaging term used to describe what happens when modern people are gripped by *me*, by viral ideas kept alive by Asherah—like Nazism and the desire to wear "Bart Simpson t-shirts." But this analysis does not make sense even in Stephenson's own terms. In the first place, *me* were prerational. In the second place, the victims of Snow Crash become robots, blind slaves, not irrationalists. Finally, many viral ideas are indistinguishable from cultural innovations, even when they appear as evil technical improvements in the means for genocide, or as consumer items coughed up by (what Donald Barthelme called) "the leading edge of the trash phenomenon," or in the currents of ideas eddying in the air that we pick up from culture's wideband babbling broadcast. In short, what Stephenson calls irrational is the very same stuff out of which he fashions his hiphop postmodern cyberpunk tale: fifteen year-old skateboarding Mercuries, religious franchises, city-state burbclaves, pizza delivery, sexually transmitted viruses, a terrorist with a personal nuclear warhead strapped to his motorcycle and "Poor Impulse Control" tattooed on his head, designer drug microcode, and charismatic leaders . . . these too are viral ideas that get enfolded into the noise of *Snow Crash*.

The inability of *Snow Crash* to confront its own metaphysics, the spiritual transcendence it conjures only to banish, comes from the fashionable unwillingness to grant any credence to narratives of metaphysics, even while so much of postmodern culture apparently yearns for it (as the literature and pronouncements about cyberspace persistently hint). We can understand this reluctance, not just on the basis of Stephenson's proud heritage from a clan of itinerant hard scientists and engineers, nomad rationalists, but as part of our more general suspicion of mystical ideas. After all, as controlling, essentializing, and privileged discourses, metaphysical constructions have done much harm throughout history, and therefore seem most worthy of resistance and radical skepticism. Yet the turn has been taken: either we are only primitives disguised as rational postmoderns and we are fooling ourselves, or we are trying to tell ourselves something that we are trained to ignore.

Stephenson will not consider the metaphysical side of the binarism for the same reasons that Gibson in subsequent novels (*Count Zero, Mona Lisa Overdrive*) drops his suggestion in *Neuromancer* that

Wintermute/Neuromancer became God and exited the system, and that Pynchon cannot pursue his playful invention of the ghosts and the Puncutron Machine in *Vineland*: We will not let them. Long habits of associating transcendence with essentializing beliefs (mistakenly), and essentializing beliefs with intolerant and destructive movements to exclude and expunge alternatives, have made us blind to our own inadmissible tendencies and yearnings, effaced and buried in our own essentializing denial. "Metaphysics" is the bad word of postmodern academia. "Religion" is unthinkable. Yet, if we attend to this late postmodern cybernetic literature and our own irrational pronouncements about the visions and yearnings it has induced in us, it becomes clear that our most interesting literature is slowly leading us, willy-nilly, into considerations of matters that were recently worthy only of contempt or marginalization in academia: that there may be more here than a mere babble of words, more than a relativizing ethos, more than congeries of bodies, energy, and information unfolding blindly in space and time.[57]

57. Part of this paper appears as "Voyage to Eudoxia: The Emergence of a New Postrational Epistemology," *SubStance* 71/72 (1993): 38–49. A French version appears in *TLE (Théorie, Littérature, Enseignement)* 11 (1993): 42–51. It was originally delivered to the *Colloque sur Épistémocritique et Cognition* in Paris, March 1992. A shorter companion piece suggests that a precursor or analogy of our present-day anticipation of cyberspace in utopian/apocalyptic imaginings can be found in the transformation of Jewish culture with the fall of the Temple and the rise of Talmudic discourse: "Transcendence at the Interface," in *Thinking Robots, an Aware Internet, and Cyberpunk Librarians*, ed. R. Bruce Miller and Milton T. Wolf (Chicago: LITA Proceedings, 1992), pp. 127–136.

Cyberspace and the
Technological Real

Michelle Kendrick

Cyberspace must be one of the most contested words in contemporary culture. Wherever the term appears, it becomes the subject of speculation and controversy, as critics and proponents argue over its function and future. This tug of war over the terrain of cyberspace both inside and outside the academy, the insistent need to name and know this cultural space, however, has generated more confusion and revealed more paradoxes than it has created clarity. Cyberspace is described, alternately, as "rational" (created and mediated by machines and mathematics) or "irrational" (mystical, performative, and cognitively dissonant), and its effects on humans are described in similarly binary terms: cyberspace is either a space for radical liberation of the self from the body or one that simply evokes the same old assumptions and values of Western metaphysics.

What most critics and defenders of cyberspace implicitly agree on, however, is that cyberspace exists, in one form or another, and that electronically mediated experience marks a decisive break in humankind's relationship to technology. I challenge both assumptions. Cyberspace does not exist as a coherent, technologically created spatial arena but as the discursive site of ideological struggles to define the relationship between technology and subjectivity. In this sense, it is *both* an imaginary projection of the idealized *telos* of technologically mediated existence *and* the latest instance of the technological interventions in human subjectivity that, I argue, always have structured definitions of the human. Cyberspace, therefore, is a cultural conjunction of fictions, projections, and anxieties that exemplify the ways in which technology intervenes in our subjectivity. But the intervention of technology in our "selves" is hardly a new, postmodern phenomenon; rather, technology has always been an affective agent in subjectivity. There is a dialogic relationship between humans and their technology that I shall call the "technological real."

Before this dialogic relationship can be examined, however, a heuristic notion of subjectivity must be described that does not exclude technological processes and artifacts as ontologically antecedent to the human. My description of subjectivity therefore seeks to interrogate and integrate two current discourses: postmodernism and Marxist-feminism. On the one hand, postmodernists critique the idea of an essential, unified, and coherent subject that exists prior to social, cultural, and historical interventions. Many theorists (Lacan, Althusser, and Derrida among them) posit instead a fragmented, partial, shifting subjectivity that is contingent on our entry into language. Because language is radically undetermined, the nature of the sign-signified relationship is never fixed, and meaning is continually deferred. The subject, as constituted through language, is, therefore, always unstable. On the other hand, some feminists and Marxists have labeled this description of subjectivity nihilistic, primarily because it threatens to erode political efficacy and the possibility of agency. Such critics want to preserve, somehow, a sense of self which, although historically interpellated, retains the possibility of effective political action. These seemingly conflicting discourses, I would suggest, are not mutually exclusive; subjectivity is a complex construction of "working fictions" which, although constructed, partial, and shifting, do work. That is, such fictions can constitute a reliable basis, at once dialogic and contingent, for political agency. In this sense, I would invoke Bruno Latour who, when interrogated about truth claims in science, replied, "I know it's true; I want to know how it's made." The making of subjectivity, then, is not a metaphor; construction requires tools, and technology, in innumerable local ways, provides the tools that aid in constantly reconstructing notions of identity that are always and already marked by radical interventions.

In this regard, the technological real may be described as a symbiotic and contentious—hence dialogic—relationship between the human and the machine. To begin to understand the significance of the technological real is to recognize that subjectivity is always in the process of being reconstructed by the technologies—material and semiotic—which it purports merely to manipulate. In this respect, any subjectivity or identity— any sense of a pretechnological reality or a reality distinct from or prior to technological interventions—can be only imaginary. The technological real, therefore, describes the inextricability of embodied identity and technology in the construction of working fictions of subjectivity.

The advent of technologies that tend to celebrate rather than obfuscate the fact that they intervene in subjectivity, however, necessarily produces widespread anxieties about the coherence of the self. At the end of the twentieth century, these anxieties have in part been redirected and assuaged by the invention of cyberspace—that is, by the rhetoric of cyberspace, which (re)defines subjectivity in relation to technology and, simultaneously, creates an imaginary space, behind the computer screen, that both exploits and denies the reality of the technological real, the multiple interventions that compose an always provisional and dialogic subjectivity.

It is, therefore, no surprise to read so many manifestos of "cyber-liberation" by those involved in promoting the sale and dissemination of computer technologies.[1] Cyberspace fictions regularly channel anxieties regarding technology into romanticized notions of a reconfigured subjectivity that represents the triumph of the algorithmic mind over a physical body that refuses to be fully computed.[2] Shifting the focus from the constructed nature of subjectivity to the "need" for technological enhancement, such fictions create a desire to be connected, a desire not to be left behind on the information

1. I offer a couple examples from the proceedings of Virtual Reality '91. Ted Nelson, of Autodesk, Inc., opened his talk with this line: "We meet to celebrate the new church of Virtual Reality." He waxed eloquent over the possibilities and concluded, "Every new dimension, every new visualizing tool, enhances our perception and realization and understanding." Norman M. Godfarb, is quoted by T. B. Coull, vice president of marketing for Sense8 Corporation, as saying, "Broadly defined, virtual reality describes an interactive computer system that is so fast and intuitive that the computer disappears from the mind of the user, leaving the computer-generated environment as the reality." (All from *Beyond the Vision: The Technology, Research, and Business of Virtual Reality*, proceedings of Virtual Reality '91: Second Annual Conference on Virtual Reality, Artificial Reality, and Cyberspace, San Francisco, September 23–25, 1991.)

2. These claims persist, despite the ease with which they can be dismantled. It is, for instance, hard to imagine computer-driven "interactive democracy" when a recent Harris poll showed that less than half the "general population had ever heard of the Internet, [one of the most touted of possible "cyberspaces"] and fewer than 20 percent had a reasonable understanding of it." Virtual Reality (the cyberspace technology that promises the most) is still a nascent technology, with cartoon graphics and jerky, time-lag movement. The University of Washington's Human Interface Technology Lab, to offer one example, recently put on "GreenSpace," which organizers described as "a history-making, trans-Pacific immersive communications medium." Seemingly unable to think of anything more interesting to do, participants from Seattle "virtually" communicated with participants from Japan on a joint venture to swat virtual "stylized" insects with hands shaped like ping-pong paddles.

superhighway. To escape the anxieties of being violated by an "in-human" technology, therefore, becomes (paradoxically) a process of producing the desire to desire more technological intervention in order to become more fully human. Cyberspace, therefore, is written by many as a new reality, in which technology actively—but safely—intervenes in subjectivity precisely to enhance it. That is, some idealized sense of a supraphysical, masculinized, and disembodied subjectivity is preserved.

Cyberspace thus is represented as intervening in our minds and bodies in a vaguely holistic fashion, not in the localized and multivalent ways in which real life assaults us. Behind the computer screen, we are to believe, this reconfigured relationship between human and machine creates a utopia of democracy, a place where the mutability of subjectivity leads only to euphoria and excess. However reassuring this imaginary vision may seem, it represses the implications of the technological real in an attempt to reinscribe the myth of a coherent identity that exists outside and prior to the technologies which create cyberspace. In this sense, cyberspace erases the material effects of virtual technologies on subjectivity. It presents the technological real as a matter of conscious choice, a decision to use or manipulate software that we can turn on and off at will. More specifically, the discourse of cyberspace suggests that humans control the technological interventions that are constantly (re)constructing our subjectivity. In this respect, cyberspace, in imagining a spaceless, timeless, and bodiless "presence," simultaneously rewrites and disrupts traditional notions of subjectivity, calling attention to the coherence of subjectivity as a fiction, yet offering itself as the actualizing of that fiction. This repressed recognition places cyberspace in a precarious position—it is always undercutting the coherent subject of Western metaphysics that it assumes and reinscribes as its conceptual foundation.

To understand more fully the dialectical effects of cyberspace, to see how it can both reinscribe and erase traditional notions of subjectivity, one must understand the historical genealogy of theories of technology. These theories are labeled in a variety of discipline-specific ways; I will begin by describing briefly the vocabulary of philosopher Andrew Feenberg, who emphasizes the distinction between "instrumental" and "substantive" theories of technology, then demonstrate the ways in which virtual technologies confound such attempts to define technology separately from its interventions in subjectivity and culture. My purpose, in this regard, is to suggest how theories of technology become implicated in the metaphysics of cyberspace, reproducing, in particular, the gendered conceptions of mind and body, human and machine that continue to be played out in the seemingly postmodern world of the Internet.

Instrumental theory presents itself as the common sense or rational theory of technology; it treats technology as a tool that is always subservient to values established in other cultural spheres. As Feenberg describes it, "a hammer is a hammer, a steam turbine is a steam turbine, and such tools are useful in any social context."[3] From this perspective, for example, the nuclear bomb could be viewed as ontologically value neutral, because outside of its specific contexts of (potential) use, it is no more or less (im)moral than a screwdriver. In contrast, substantive theories of technology, such as those of Jacques Ellul and Martin Heidegger, among others, attribute an autonomous cultural force or logic to technology which overrides traditional or competing values. In this view, technology's effects on culture and nature are more significant than its ostensible goals. Technology is, at once, viewed as systemic and disruptive—it affects cultures in ways that are unpredictable and often unmanageable. The nuclear bomb, for instance, might be seen as the historical instigator and a governing principle of "nuclear culture," with effects that go beyond its immediate functions as weapon and deterrent.

Despite the claims made for the new computer technologies, theorists of cyberspace generally recode either the instrumental or substantive theories of technology, even as they proclaim the revolutionary or transcendental nature of electronic media. Proponents view these new technologies as further advances in a progressivist revolutionary development, as tools which can be usefully applied to education, entertainment, or medicine. On the one hand, Brenda Laurel insists that culture will use the new communication media that come with cyberspace, "as we have used every previous medium, to conjure up transformative powers, to propel us beyond the boundaries of our minds and push our cultural evolution into new territories."[4] On the other hand, sceptics emphasize the systemic nature of the new technology and decry what they see as (yet another) technological take-over of the human by machines. Neil Postman, to take only one example, sees computer technologies as the agents of a dystopian future: "We have relinquished control,

3. Andrew Feenberg, *Critical Theory of Technology* (New York: Oxford University Press, 1991).

4. As quoted in Howard Rheingold, *Virtual Reality* (New York: Summit Press, 1991), p. 385.

which in the case of the computer means that we may, without excessive remorse, pursue ill-advised and even inhuman goals because the computer can accomplish them."[5] Postman's writing resonates with nostalgia for a return to a time when humans controlled technology, not the other way around. Significantly, though, Laurel and Postman share the basic presupposition that there is an a priori human subject distinct from technology who will either use or be used by it.[6] This unified, Cartesian subject either controls the neutral tools of technology and uses them to advance (almost always) his interests and values, or is reduced, in Heidegger's terms, to a "standing reserve" by a powerful controlling technological system.[7] In either case, technology is cordoned off rather than interrogated, given a curiously autonomous and self-propelling logic of its own.

In arguing that virtual technologies are revolutionary in their effects on human subjectivity, proponents of cyberspace draw on traditional Cartesian distinctions of the mind and body to argue that the self is bodiless and, indeed, that its abstract nature is precisely what allows it to be seen as unique, unified, and coherent. In an important sense, therefore, cyberspace both invokes and promises to transcend what, in fact, does not exist—the unified and self-identical subject who is distinct from his or her body and from the technological context of culture. David Tomas, in his article on the movement from Euclidian space to cyberspace, writes that new computer technologies will eventually allow us to "overthrow the sensorial and organic architecture of the human body, this by dis-

5. Neil Postman, *Technopoly: The Surrender of Culture to Technology* (New York: Random House, 1992), p. 114.

6. The transcendence promised (over space, time, bodies, race, and gender) in the various readings of these fictions demonstrates that many cultural commentators on cyberspace reinscribe as a basic assumption a division of reality from technology. For example, one phenomenon of cyberspace which is touted as "new" is that it is or will be "interactive." Joseph Henderson of Dartmouth's Interactive Media Laboratory quotes Timothy Leary to make this point: "Most Americans have been living in Virtual Reality since the proliferation of television. All cyberspace will do is make the experience interactive instead of passive" (in *Beyond the Vision* [above, n. 1], p. 89). Implicit in this logic is a definition of technology, prior to cyberspace, as an array of static tools that are acted upon by their users but do not interact, do not evoke response, or act reciprocally. Such a view posits an a priori technologically unmediated reality peopled by Cartesian subjects who act independently of technology. Only through this logic can cyberspace be read, as it often is, as a Hegelian synthesis and, therefore, as a means to transcend the material conditions—the very technologies that bring it into being.

7. Martin Heidegger, *The Question Concerning Technology and Other Essays* (New York: Garland Publishing, 1977).

embodying and reformatting its sensorium in powerful, computer-generated, digitalized spaces."[8] Tomas's prediction rests on a traditional vision of subjectivity, specifically, the assumption that what is to be overthrown is a subject which is knowable in full and open to "reformatting" in a place beyond the body. In dismissing the body as simply a container, so much "architecture," from which to transplant the "sensorium," Tomas reproduces the age-old philosophical move of separating the devalued body from the mind.[9]

These dualistic views of technology and subjectivity, from Feenberg to Tomas, cannot adequately convey the complexity of the relationship between humans and machines. The subject is now, and has been historically, constructed—embodied by and against the technologies of his/her time. In this sense, technology actively intervenes in the construction and social reformulations of subjectivity; so, specific technological interactions, "assistance," and disruptions cause subsequent reformulations of one's sense of self. At the same time, the repressed recognition that technologies do intervene in our bodies produces the desire to distinguish ourselves from these interventions, to imagine a self that is not subject to prosthetic assistance or its corollaries: disease, decay, and death. The process of subjectivity cannot be separate from an embodied experience that impels both the denial of the technological real and the idealization of the disembodied self as a kind of fetish.

In contrast, a more complex view of subjectivity must examine the intersections among narratives of identity; material, social, and psychic interactions with technology; and the experience of embodiment. In positioning subjectivity as connected in a complex manner to the body, I do not mean to evoke simply another layer of abstraction, a generalized notion of "the body." This concept has been critiqued thoroughly by feminist theorists such as Elizabeth Grosz

8. David Tomas, "Old Rituals for New Space: Rites de Passage and William Gibson's Cultural Model of Cyberspace," in *Cyberspace: First Steps,* ed. Michael Benedikt (Cambridge, Mass. MIT Press, 1991), p. 32.

9. Tomas is far from alone in proposing a stable subjectivity open to reproduction and reconstitution. Two proponents of Virtual Reality, Eric Gullichen and Randy Walser, claim that cyberspace will not "merely provide new experiences," but "will change what humans perceive themselves to be, at a very fundamental and personal level." Specifically, this radical (re)inventing of the human being will hinge on two factors: the relegating of the body to the status of "meat" and the accompanying malleability of subjectivity that a "bodiless" entity is presumed to have. Gullicen and Walser thus offer a prophecy of "alternative personalities," which will have "social, economic, artistic, technical and ethical consequences every bit as significant as [one's] 'original' personality" (quoted in Rheingold, *Virtual Reality* [above n. 4], p. 191). Gullichen and Walser also see the subject as open to replication in full, somewhere without the body.

and Susan Bordo, who suggest that the body, as an abstraction, is ahistorical, erasing critical differences because it evokes notions of sameness, similarity, and continuity.[10] The most appropriate critical response to those approaches that celebrate the displacement of historical bodies into "the body" is to ask, paraphrasing Foucault, "Which one?" To fully understand the implications of celebrating disembodiment, one must be develop an understanding of the responsibility incurred by a recognition of embodiment and the materiality of specific bodies: sense perceptions, proprioception, muscle memory, other biological functions, and physical manifestations of emotional effects. Furthermore, as Foucault and others have demonstrated, the experience of embodiment exists in a dialectical relationship with social, cultural, and historical discourses and is invariably implicated in a complex ecological as well as political environment. Pierre Bourdieu suggests as much in his concept of the habitus, which he defines as "embodied history, internalized as a second nature and so forgotten as history—[it] is the active presence of the whole past of which it is a product." For Bourdieu, common practices and representations are determined through the dialectical relationship between the body and a structured organization of space and time.[11]

It is this "dialectical relationship" that constructs subjectivity, the complex interactions and relations among the materiality of technology, bodies, and narratives of identity that constitute the subject. This is a proposal at once simple and yet remarkably hard to comprehend. One has only to consider how fully implicated one's life is in current technologies—from the medicines we take that cure our illnesses, to our contact lenses, to the cars that enable us to live and work and play in a wide geographic area—to begin to recognize the pervasiveness of this claim. Technology affects the social and individual conception of the self, the parameters that enable "changes" in the self, even the social, political, and personal possibilities that subjects, as agents, can envision. This is not to say that technology determines social or personal identity in any systemic manner, nor is it to buy into simply another version of the substantive theory of technology. The technological real forces us instead to recognize the complexity and materiality of subjectivity;

10. See Elizabeth Grosz, *Volatile Bodies: Towards a Corporeal Feminism* (Bloomington: Indiana University Press, 1994); and Susan Bordo, *Unbearable Weight: Feminism, Western Culture, and the Body* (Berkeley: University of California Press, 1993).

11. Pierre Bourdieu, *Outline of a Theory of Practice*, trans. Richard Nice (Cambridge: Cambridge University Press, 1977), p. 56.

only through examining such complexity can specific sites of construction be examined and understood.

To recognize technology's specific interventions in subjectivity is to admit that notions of identity are context-specific in ways that call attention to what Don Ihde has called our "doubled desire" regarding technology: to master technology in order to use it to reshape our environment in order to produce a "natural" bounty, which presumably will take us back to a prelapsarian world, and thereby render technology invisible.[12] In his essay in this collection, Robert Markley argues that cyberspace is a prime example of this doubling of desire: "Cyberspace promises to take us beyond the interventions of technology—ironically, only by repressing those interventions, by effacing the technologies on which it depends."[13] It is precisely this attempt to erase its technological construction that allows cyberspace to erase the body, to invoke implicitly and explicitly a philosophical tradition that insistently devalues the material in order to create an idealized, ahistorical notion of the self. This tendency to erase the body has important implications for both current philosophizing about cyberspace and for a specifically feminist critique of the dangers and potential of virtual technologies.

Many critics of cyberspace—Michael Heim and Steve Shaviro among them—adopt Gottfried Leibniz as the philosopher who is most useful in theorizing the problems of subjectivity in cyberspace.[14] For these critics, Leibniz's monadology offers a philosophical basis for the simulations created by computer technologies. Leibnizian monads, writes Heim, "are nonphysical, psychical substances" that operate from a solitary, omniscient position.[15] Monads, as cohesive but bodiless entities, seem to represent precisely the experience (or more accurately the *imagined* experience) of cyberspace: they present themselves as expressions of pure desire. In contrast, I suggest that it is precisely the Leibnizian idealized erasure of the body—repressing its materiality into the form of the monad—that makes his philosophy problematic in theorizing the complica-

---

12. Don Ihde, *Technology and the Lifeworld: From Garden to Earth* (Bloomington: Indiana University Press, 1990) pp. 75–76.

13. Robert Markley, "Boundaries: Mathematics, Alienation, and the Metaphysics of Cyberspace," *Configurations* 3 (1994): p. 503.

14. See Michael Heim *The Metaphysics of Virtual Reality* (New York: Oxford University Press, 1993) pp. 83–108; and Steve Shaviro's manuscript "Doom Patrols," available by ftp at: ftp://ftp.u.washington.edu/public/shaviro/doom.html.

15. Heim, *Metaphysics of Virtual Reality,* p. 97.

tions of computer technologies. Notions of subjectivity, however abstract, are always and inescapably embodied. The bodiless entity that hypothetically exists in cyberspace depends, in myriad ways, on the referent of the corporeal body in front of the computer. The relationship between the embodied user, the creation of "alternate" subjectivities in cyberspace, and the technology of the computer, is tightly intermeshed; and evoking Leibniz can reduce the complexity by bracketing the body, allowing its displacement into the seemingly unencumbered, desiring intelligence (described by Heim and Shaviro), and encouraging the imaginary erasure of technology as the constitutive force of the simulation. In this respect, I would explicitly counter the move to adopt Leibniz as the philosopher of choice for cyberspace and instead suggest an alternate history that factors embodiment into descriptions of subjectivity.[16] In this sense, a more useful philosopher of subjectivity might be David Hume, who calls into question the metaphysical presuppositions of monadological views of cyberspace.

Hume, in *A Treatise of Human Nature* (1739), posits subjectivity and identity as "working" fictions.[17] Countering Descartes's notion of the mind as infinitely divisible and separate from the physical body, Hume suggests that the human consists of a flux of distinct sensory perceptions, continued through time and widely various. However hard individuals try to make sense of the distinct and unconnected nature of their sense perceptions, they are unable to process—without relying on fictions of causal connection—the continual movement and variety of their existence. Hume describes what is effectively a dialogic relationship between our awareness of the chaos of sensory perceptions and the putative stability of fictions of identity:

> however at one instant we may consider the related succession [of perceptions] as variable or interrupted, we are sure the next to ascribe to it a perfect identity, and regard it as invariable and uninterrupted. . . . Thus we feign the continu'd existence of the perceptions of our senses, to remove the interrup-

16. Katherine Hayles's essay in this volume, "Boundary Disputes: Homeostasis, Reflexivity and the Foundations of Cybernetics," intelligently critiques the notion of cyberliberation from the constraints of the body. Notions of disembodiment, she argues, can occlude the history of distinctions between form and matter, which will continue to be important in the development, use, and instantiation of new technologies. She asks, "Is it necessary to insist, once again, that embodiment is not an option but a necessity in order for life to exist?"

17. David Hume, *A Treatise of Human Nature* (Oxford: Clarendon Press, 1951).

tion; and run into the notion of soul, and self, and substance, to disguise the variation.[18]

The process of crafting the fiction of "soul, and self, and substance," Hume argues, is founded on memory. Memory is, in a very real sense, truly the process of re-membering—yoking the temporal sequence of distinct sensory perceptions and the beliefs and ideas that they inspire through notions of *resemblance* and *causation*. For Hume, resemblance (the linking of like perceptions) and causation (the attributing of cause and effect relations to external and unconnected events) are tendencies of the mind which become the habit of identity. This is, of course, a narrative process. The narration of past becomes the foundation for present and future perceptions of our sense of self.

Gilles Deleuze, in the preface to *Empiricism and Subjectivity,* writes a brilliantly succinct description of Hume's philosophy:

> We start with atomic parts, but these atomic parts have transitions, passages, "tendencies," which circulate from one to another. These tendencies give rise to habits. Isn't this the answer to the question "what are we?" We are habits, nothing but habits—the habit of saying "I." Perhaps there is no more striking answer to the problem of the Self.[19]

The answer of the self, in this respect, consists of an embodied entity who exists in space and time. These terms—identity, embodiment, space, time, and narration—crucial to Hume's argument, need to be seen in a nontraditional manner, as terms which resist efforts to collapse them into philosophical postulates or render them (in the case of the monadology) irrelevant. The subject exists through time, in memory, and by means of the "habit" of connecting perceptions in such a manner that they continually reinscribe the fiction of a stable identity. The spaces of sensory impression, in contrast to the imaginary spaces behind the computer screen, are proprioceptive spaces. Hume assumes, always, a primacy of the body which is inescapable. "We may well ask," writes Hume, "what causes induce us to believe in the existence of body? but it is in vain to ask, whether there be a body or not? that is a point, which we must take for granted in all our reasonings."[20] There can be no dis-

18. Ibid., p. 254.

19. Gilles Deleuze, *Empiricism and Subjectivity* (New York: Columbia University Press, 1991), p. x.

20. Hume, *Treatise of Human Nature,* p. 87.

missing the space of our bodies, which perceive and sense, which gather the data on which to assemble our habitual fictions.

It is crucial to emphasize that the stakes of this debate entail far more than mere philosophical musings. As materialist feminists have demonstrated, the erasing of specific situated bodies, through abstractions of disembodiment, serves primarily to bolster the privilege of those in Western culture with unmarked bodies—primarily white upper- or upper-middle-class males. As Donna Haraway suggests, "we need the power of modern critical theories of how meanings and bodies get made, not in order to deny meaning and bodies, but in order to live in meanings and bodies that have a chance for the future."[21] Cyberspatial visions of selves unconstrained by bodies, of a radical unmarking of situated identities, appropriate the rhetoric of the liberation of self from the body to foster an idealized notion of a fluid, undifferentiated identity. Shaviro contends that in cyberspace "selves are no longer constrained by rules of unity and organic form; you can adopt whatever pseudonym you want. We are all the same in cyberspace, and anyone can be replaced by anyone else." To buy into this rhetoric is to lose sight of the specificity of located subjectivities within a cultural, historical context and also, crucially, to lose sight of the ways in which this context is constantly being reproduced by technological interventions.[22] In this respect, to recognize subjectivity as an effect of the technological real is not to sink into relativism nor to level socioeconomic and biological differences but to provide a means to critique the logic that reduces the relationships between humankind and technology to the sets of binaries that I have critiqued.

My emphasis on the ways in which cyberspace reaches back to Leibniz to promote an idealized vision of electronically mediated experience and thereby to disembody subjectivity can be understood as a characteristic response to the advent of new media, which we persist in trying to fit into traditional paradigms of knowledge, such as mind-body dualism. Thirty years ago Marshall McLuhan argued that the content of any new medium is precisely the old medium that it has replaced. In this sense, cyberspace becomes a key site in a self-consciously postmodern culture for individual articulation and repression of the antagonisms of class and

21. Donna J. Haraway, *Simians, Cyborgs, and Women: The Reinvention of Nature* (New York: Routledge, 1990), p. 187.

22. Susan Bordo writes about a similar impulse to level through "postmodern" shifting of "subjectivity": "Instead of distinctions, endless differences reign—an undifferentiated pastiche of differences, a grab bag in which no items are assigned any more importance or centrality than any others" (*Unbearable Weight* [above, n. 10], p. 258).

gender that it claims to transcend. The privileges of gender, class, and race persist in the ostensibly unmarked arena of cyberspace; experiments with, say, gender in cyberspace emerge less as alternatives to the complexity of embodied subjectivity than as unstable sites that erupt into crisis when the role-playing that some virtual spaces encourage comes up against the inequalities and power differentials of Real Life.

Allucquere Rosanne Stone, in her article "Will the Real Body Please Stand Up?" argues that cyberspace is collapsing nature into technology.[23] "On the nets," she claims, "*warranting,* or grounding, a persona in a physical body is meaningless" (p. 84), and she goes on to celebrate the "decoupling [of] the body and the subject." But even as she invokes the notion of a coherent, reproducible subject that is not context specific, Stone also offers examples that demonstrate moments of intense anxiety regarding the putative decoupling of body and subject. I should like to focus briefly on one of these, the story of "Julie," an older disabled woman who was known to the Internet community only by her textual presence. Julie, apparently, had an enormous effect on those who interacted with her. Stone tells us, "in the intimate electronic companionships that can develop . . . on-line . . . Julie's women friends shared their deepest troubles, and she offered them advice—advice which changed their lives" (p. 83). When information was leaked that "Julie" was actually an able-bodied middle-aged male psychiatrist, the general reaction was of disbelief and outrage. Stone recounted a typical response from one woman: "'I felt raped. . . . I felt my deepest secrets had been violated'" (p. 83). It is no accident that these women used rape discourse and metaphors to articulate their sense of violation. If, explicitly, these interactions seemed to be about confiding, sharing, and advice, *implicitly* they reflect a process of constructing subjectivity. Within this process, which was mediated through the technology of the computer, the body was offered as foundational, as a territory, or site, of trust. The women who corresponded with Julie offered, as part of the process, their own embodied subjectivity as women, in an economy of cyclical construction which established working fictions of subjectivity on the Internet. Far from their bodies being decoupled, and hence meaningless, the women's reactions to Julie's betrayal demonstrate an intense embodied relation to one another—even in cyberspace. These women

---

23. Allucquere Rosanne Stone, "Will the Real Body Please Stand Up?: Boundary Stories about Virtual Cultures," in Benedikt, *Cyberspace* (above, n. 8), pp. 81–118. Specific page citations to this work will be made in the text.

participated in the construction of a discursive subjectivity, and they had the expectation of an embodiment that would correspond to that subject—an elderly, disabled woman sharing sincerely felt emotions with them.

The expectation of bodies *somewhere* in a specific context at once gestures to a certain primacy of the body and to the expectation that technology, in this case, mediates *between* specific embodied realities, specific stable identities, rather than creating alternate realities. What is demonstrated in the "betrayal" is how technology intervenes, in powerful ways, in the construction of working fictions of subjectivities. The anger and anxiety registered by the women also suggests that cyberspace has the potential to disturb, to use Hume's language, our sense of resemblance and causality. The women thought that they recognized Julie as a similar subject, or at least as a particular kind of subject—a kind, wise, and disabled woman. Thus, while these fictions of cyberspace assuage anxieties by suggesting that once we "jack out" of the matrix we will return to a coherent subjectivity—as a colleague recently put it, "we are only fluid and multiplicitous until someone unplugs the computer"—they also have the potential to disrupt narratives of causality and resemblance. When events such as Julie's betrayal occur, they reveal the constructed nature of subjectivity in intensely disturbing ways. Stone tells us that, as a result of the discovery that "Julie" was a man, several women "went so far as to repudiate the genuine gains they had made in their personal and emotional lives" (p. 83). Their repudiations suggest both that the process of constructing subjectivity through the mediation of technology can yield genuine gains and that recognizing this process of construction can be disturbing enough, in many instances, to inspire denial of those gains.

If the story of Julie suggests the insecurities that lie behind our associations of self and body, then another well-known example of gender bending in cyberspace reveals the ways in which power, privilege, and hostility can appropriate the play of differences in an imaginary realm of supposedly fluid identities. Julian Dibbell, in his article "A Rape in Cyberspace," recounts a particularly complex example of the ways in which cyberspace recodes and is structured by the complex relations between technology and subjectivity.[24] Dibbell's story, like Stone's, describes technologically mediated in-

24. Julian Dibbell, "A Rape in Cyberspace, or How an Evil clown, a Haitian Trickster Spirit, Two Wizards, and Cast of Dozen Turned a Database into a Society," originally published in the *Village Voice,* December 21, 1993. Electronically redistributed on the Internet and not-for-profit bulletin boards.

teractions, in this case, within a computer database named Lamb-damoo (MOO stands for a multi-user domain, object oriented). In brief, Lambdamoo is a shared computer space which allows multiple users to interact in a (textually described) communal environment, in this case, a large mystical mansion. Users log on to the imaginary space and write descriptions of characters who become their Lambdamoo personas.

In describing the "rape" that occurred in Lambdamoo, Dibbell recounts two versions of the facts, one from Virtual Reality (VR) and one from real life (RL). In Dibbell's Virtual Reality version, Mr. Bungle, a "fat oleaginous, Bisquick-faced clown,"

> . . . commenced his assault entirely unprovoked, at or about 10 p.m. Pacific Standard Time. That he began by using his voodoo doll to force one of the room's occupants to sexually service him in a variety of more or less conventional ways. That this victim was legba, a Haitian trickster spirit of indeterminate gender, brown-skinned and wearing an expensive pearl grey suit. (p. 37)

To assault legba, Mr. Bungle used a voodoo doll subprogram which allows users to "appropriate" and control, temporarily, the character of another player. In this manner, Mr. Bungle "took over" the character of legba and subjected him/her to sexually explicit acts. In fact, although legba was of indeterminate gender, Mr. Bungle's assault was "a brand of degradation reserved for the embodied female" (p. 37). However,

> no hideous or trickster spirits appear in the RL version of the incident, no voodoo dolls or wizard guns, indeed no rape at all as any RL court of law has yet defined it. The actors in the drama were university students for the most part, and they sat rather undramatically before computer screens the entire time. . . . no bodies touched. Whatever physical interaction occurred consisted of a mingling of electronic signals. (p. 37)

Further complicating the problem of defining the relationship between virtual violence and real life is the fact that, as Dibbell explains, the "rape" in cyberspace was a public act. Other users were logged on and "witnessed" Mr. Bungle's abuse. Reactions in the virtual community, as we shall see, ranged from anger and shock to amusement and indifference. A controversy ensued which centered around how best to respond to such an event. Should Mr. Bungle be "toaded"—eliminated from the MUD (multi-user domain)—or would some kind of community censure be the appropriate response?

Dibbell juxtaposes the two versions of this rape in cyberspace in order to complicate the notion of "alternate realities." He offers this story, with all its confusion and emotion, as a countermeasure to what he calls "the techno-utopian ecstasies of West Coast cyberhippies" and as a place to begin exploring the *relationship* between the physical body and its cyberspatial projection (p. 37). What is important is the idea of relationship. The word suggests a crucial fact about cyberspace: MUDs are not places of alternate subjectivities, of a transcending of one's social and biological identity, but of simultaneous subjectivities. There are always at least two subject positions, neither separated nor identical, for each user. "Julie" was, at once, an old and disabled woman and a middle-aged able-bodied man. Mr. Bungle was a "Bisquick-faced clown" and also, at the same time, an unknown person operating a keyboard. Crises such as the "rape" emphasize the slippage and cyber-schizophrenia that result when the relationship between the user and the projected persona is brought into the foreground.

The reactions to the assault seem similar to the ones Stone recounts. Other characters in Lambdamoo were angry, disgusted, and bewildered. The reaction of legba (in real life a female doctoral candidate) illustrates, I believe, the contradictory ways in which technologically mediated "assault" may affect subjectivity. Legba's written contribution to the discussion in Lambdamoo of how to punish Mr. Bungle demonstrates the slippage. It is a strange mixture of outrage and annoyance:

> Mostly voodoo dolls are amusing, and mostly I tend to think that restrictive measures around here cause more trouble than they prevent. But I also think that Mr. Bungle was being a vicious, vile fuckhead, and I . . . want his sorry ass scattered from #17 to the Cinder Pile. I'm not calling for policies, trials, or better jails. I'm not sure what I'm calling for. Virtual castration, if I could manage it. Mostly, [this type of thing] doesn't happen here. Mostly, perhaps I thought it wouldn't happen to me. Mostly, I trust people to conduct themselves with some veneer of civility. Mostly, I want his ass. (p. 38)

The female user who created the legba persona is clearly outraged. In places, her rhetoric reproduces classic rape discourse, mingling anger, confusion, denial, and disbelief. On one level her response calls for "virtual castration," a bodily retaliation for an assault that, though electronic and textual, is coded in terms of the body. Her anger testifies, once again, to the persistence of the "real" body in cyberspace and confirms her feelings that an assault on her avatar is somehow an assault on her body and on her embodied identity. The doubleness, the simultaneity, of legba, the Haitian trickster spirit, and the woman at a keyboard are, in this moment of crisis, thrown into dramatic relief. This doubleness is reflected in her conflicted response to the "rape." Rather than reacting as though the legba persona were an alternate personality, a conscious role that she could put on or off at will, she strongly exhibits the connection, the continued complicity, of technological mediation in her sense of her "real" self.

In addition to outrage, there is another quality to her response, what Dibbell describes as an "eyeball rolling annoyance" (p. 38). This quality is evident most clearly in the sudden shift from the rape discourse—"I didn't think it would happen to me"—to her expectation that "people will act with a veneer of civility." Dibbell writes, "Where virtual reality and its conventions would have us believe that legba and Starsinger were brutally raped in their own living room, here was the victim legba scolding Mr. Bungle for a breach of 'civility.'" He accounts for such a discordant response by attributing it to the "buzzing, dissonant gap" between Virtual Reality and real life (p. 38). Another way to account for this is to read it as a disturbance, again, of an organizing principle of subjectivity— the causality without which, as Hume notes, agency cannot exist. The "eyeball rolling annoyance" of the user coupled with her discourse as rape victim show the instability of the simultaneous subject positions, the inability to rely on a coherent a priori subjectivity, predicated on a notion of control. Cyberspace discourses suggest that users can consciously construct what "else" they would be. Agency inheres in the idea of a user who can construct alternate subject positions. In the "rape" case, the user believes she is in control of the process of constructing legba, her cyberspatial projection, until she is suddenly shown—in a graphic and visceral way—that the process of constructing subjectivity is far more complicated and open to interventions than the simple cyberspatial promise of transcendence would lead one to suspect.

For instance, the person who created/is legba has no legal recourse for the "assault." The notion of causality between the act and the user's distress is denied in the social and cultural context where she is physically present. Legba has no agency; he/she cannot prosecute; no one in real life recognizes any claims about legba's identity in cyberspace. The loss of a coherent social and bodily context seems to disrupt the user/legba's ability to decipher just what happened to her "self," precisely because the cyber-rape emphasizes that the construction of subjectivity is a process of intervening social and technological forces, in many ways beyond the control or agency of the user.[25]

25. Katherine Hayles, in *Chaos Bound: Orderly Disorder in Contemporary Literature and Science* (Ithaca, N.Y.: Cornell University Press, 1990), proposes that the "loss of a stable

If cyberspace is a discursive site of ideological struggles to define the relationship between subjectivity and technology, it becomes crucial to theorize our technologies, to move beyond the visions of tools and encapsulating systems, and to recognize the multiple ways that technologies intervene in our cultural identities. For example, for feminist critics to ask how cyberspace might reproduce traditional gendered discourse is to pose an interesting and relevant question, but one that remains a subset of what are, I argue, much larger questions. How do technologies create gendered subjectivities? How do we reformulate gender in light of technological interventions? What is the history of such interventions?

To explore these questions is to take seriously a view of the subject that is more Humean than Cartesian or Leibnizian, that is, to see the gaps and lacunas between our sense perceptions and our narratives of identities and to recognize the absolute necessity of the body in producing and maintaining those foundational perceptions. It is to understand the subject not as stable, coherent, or knowable but always as process, a kind of ongoing technoproject. If one understands the subject as contingent on the experience of embodiment, then any theory that suggests a radical reconstruction or abandoning of the body must be read as part of a traditional metaphysics which, from Plato, through Descartes, to Heim, has devalued corporeal experience. Finally, and perhaps most crucially, it is to recognize the subject as context-specific and to see subjectivity as created in an always interactive environment, in which whatever we experience as true, real, and fundamental is inseparable from the technologies through which we are continually reinscribed.

context," is what marks something as simulacrum. "Cyberspace," she writes, "presupposes a radical erosion of context, for the sense that something is an original depends on its association with a unique context" (p. 276). The conflicting rhetoric of legba in cyberspace reflects such an erosion of context; it displays confusion concerning the notion of "originality," both in the sense of *original*'s meaning first and initial and in the sense of origin as the place where the violation actually occurred.

Contributors

David Brande has recently completed a book manuscript, "Technologies of Postmodernity: Ideology and Desire in Literature and Science." He has published on the fiction of Kathy Acker and is currently an instructor at Lewis and Clark College.

Richard Grusin is the director of undergraduate studies in the School of Literature, Communication, and Culture at Georgia Tech. Author of *Transcendentalist Hermeneutics: Institutional Authority and the Higher Criticism of the Bible,* he is currently at work on a book-length study of the national parks, tentatively entitled "The Reproduction of Nature: Art, Science, and the National Parks, 1864–1916."

N. Katherine Hayles, a professor of English at UCLA, is the author of *Chaos Bound: Orderly Disorder in Contemporary Literature and Science.* She is currently completing "Virtual Bodies: Evolving Materiality in Cybernetics, Literature, and Information." The implications of "constrained constructivism" are explored in her work-in-progress, "Riding the Cusp: The Interplay of Narrative with Scientific Theories."

Michelle Kendrick is the assistant director of the Center for Advanced Research Technology in the Arts and Humanities at the University of Washington. She has published articles on technology and contemporary culture in *Cultural Critique* and elsewhere and is completing a study of technology and American fiction.

Robert Markley is the Jackson Distinguished Chair of British Literature at West Virginia University. His most recent book is *Fallen Languages: Crises of Representation in Newtonian England, 1660–1740,* and he is currently completing a study entitled "Reality Effects: Gender, Science Studies, and Virtual Technologies." The article in this collection was completed while he held a Fellow-

ship for University Teachers from the National Endowment for the
Humanities.

            David Porush is the author of *The Soft Machine: Cybernetic Fiction* and numerous articles about science and
literature. His work-in-progress is "Telepathies: The End of Alphabetic Consciousness and the Advent of Virtual Reality." He is a professor of literature and communication at Rennsalaer Polytechnic
Institute.

Library of Congress Cataloging-in-Publication Data

Virtual realities and their discontents / edited by
Robert Markley.
    p.   cm.
  Revised, expanded version of the fall 1994 issue of the
JHUP journal, Configurations.
  ISBN 0-8018-5225-0 (alk. paper). — ISBN 0-8018-5226-9
(pbk. : alk. paper)
  1. Human-computer interaction. 2. Virtual reality.
I. Markley, Robert, 1952– . II. Configurations.
QA76.9.H85V55   1996
810.9'0356—dc20   95-21184